"Handling a transition well is how a leader keeps a great organization great and propels its new season to the next level. A leader in a new environment is faced with former expectations, a past legacy, and new people. Tyler Reagin addresses how to lead through intimidating new chapters with confidence and excellence. He does an incredible job preparing leaders to navigate these transitions and create confident and impactful leaders. I recommend this book as a great resource to anyone handling a transition and leading an organization or team into its next season!"

—CHAD VEACH, lead pastor of Zoe Church, Los Angeles

"For years, I've appreciated the leadership of Tyler Reagin as he has taught me to be a better person, friend, and leader to the people around me. What a privilege for any reader who gets to absorb Tyler's wisdom throughout this book. His words are seasoned with years of lived experience and will leave you feeling refreshed and ready to propel yourself forward into all the new things God has for you."

—HANNAH BRENCHER, author of *Fighting Forward* and *Come Matter Here*

"*Leading Things You Didn't Start* is a perfect resource for a whole new generation of leaders who are stepping into senior leadership and taking over top positions from their boomer and Generation X predecessors. Tyler Reagin does an impressive job outlining the key issues, and the case studies he features are worth the price of the book alone. If you're leading something you didn't start, or are about to, you need to read this book."

—CAREY NIEUWHOF, bestselling author, speaker, and podcast host

"Stepping into an organization previously directed by another leader is always a challenging opportunity. Tyler Reagin brings incredible insight and wisdom to any new leader who is seeking to help an organization move forward with its vision for its program and people. I wish I'd had this treasure thirty years ago to challenge me with important questions I should have been asking!"

—ARCHBISHOP FOLEY BEACH, Anglican Church in North America

# Leading Things
# You Didn't Start

# Leading Things You Didn't Start

## WINNING BIG WHEN YOU INHERIT PEOPLE, PLACES, AND POSSIBILITIES

### Tyler Reagin

WATERBROOK

Published in the United States by WaterBrook, an imprint of Random House, a division of Penguin Random House LLC.

WATERBROOK® and its deer colophon are registered trademarks of Penguin Random House LLC.

Library of Congress Cataloging-in-Publication Data
Names: Reagin, Tyler, author.
Title: Leading things you didn't start: winning big when you inherit people, places, and possibilities / by Tyler Reagin.
Description: First edition. | Colorado Springs: WaterBrook, 2021. | Includes bibliographical references.
Identifiers: LCCN 2020017004 | ISBN 9780525654049 (hardcover) | ISBN 9780525654056 (ebook)
Subjects: LCSH: Leadership—Religious aspects—Christianity. | Success—Religious aspects—Christianity.
Classification: LCC BV4597.53.L43 R425 2021 | DDC 253—dc23
LC record available at https://lccn.loc.gov/2020017004

Printed in Canada on acid-free paper

waterbrookmultnomah.com

2 4 6 8 9 7 5 3 1

First Edition

SPECIAL SALES
Most WaterBrook books are available at special quantity discounts when purchased in bulk by corporations, organizations, and special-interest groups. Custom imprinting or excerpting can also be done to fit special needs. For information, please email specialmarketscms@penguinrandomhouse.com.

*To Ganny and Poppy Jenkins.*
*Thanks for all the lunches and gas money that helped get me*
*through college and start my career. I miss you both.*

*And here's to my 420 SAT score in English.*
*I'm thankful I didn't let that score keep me from writing and*
*creating leadership content. Don't let things you*
*don't like define you either.*

# Contents

# Foreword

IT'S ONE THING TO START AND LEAD SOMETHING, BUT IT'S ANOTHER THING entirely to lead something you didn't start.

More than a decade ago, my wife and I took over as lead pastors of Churchome, a growing church community formerly known as the City Church. We had always known that someday we would lead the church, but someday seemed a long way off. Then, due to my father's declining health and his battle against cancer, the transition was dramatically accelerated. Within a very short time, we found ourselves at the helm of a church we loved—but one that seemed far too big for our experience or capacity.

Not only was the task itself enormous, but we were also trying to fill the shoes and follow in the footsteps of legends. My parents planted the church and functioned as its lead pastors for many years, and they were incredible leaders. They built a community that looked to them and loved them. Their impact was—and still is—felt around the world.

I remember the conflicting feelings of stepping into that role: it was exhilarating and terrifying, inspiring and intimidating, a privilege and a weight. It wasn't easy (that's an understatement), but I wouldn't change it for anything. Those years of transition were like no other season in our lives. It was a time of growth, of mistakes, of prayer, of learning, of vision, of change. As difficult as it was, the beauty has far outlasted the challenges: today the church continues to grow, thrive, and fulfill its mission.

Looking back, I realize there were many things I didn't know going into that transition—things I had to learn the hard way. I had to hit the ground running, and I tripped and fell more than I probably should have. It took me a while to get up to speed in my leadership role.

Tyler's book *Leading Things You Didn't Start* was written for precisely that reason: to help new leaders hit the ground running. From his years of experience in a wide range of leadership roles, he presents solid, practical keys to making healthy transitions while keeping the bumps and bruises to a minimum.

It's a timely message, and it could make all the difference if your organization is in the process of handing off the leadership baton—especially if *you* are the one receiving that baton. One of the marks of a healthy organization is that it has the momentum, maturity, and margin to transcend any one leader. Whether you lead a church, a business, a nonprofit, or any other organization, if you and your team can navigate the transition to new leadership, you are on your way to multigenerational success.

—JUDAH SMITH

# Section 1

## THE FOUNDATIONS FOR INHERITANCE

WHAT DEFINES GREAT LEADERS?

> Leaders are learners.
> Leaders ask great questions.
> Leaders get the best out of their people.
> Leaders go first.
> Leaders serve those around them.
> Leaders solve problems.
> Leaders develop systems.
> Leaders encourage.
> Leaders fight for the best.
> Leaders build great organizations.

When you lead at a high level for any length of time, you'll get noticed. Even if you're not a perfectly polished leadership gem . . . *yet*. Not only will you get noticed, but you'll also get opportunity—opportunity to step into a new space. A new role. A promotion.

However, most of us won't initiate something new. Most of us, when called on, will step into a leadership role that belonged to someone else. We will join a team that already exists. We will take ownership of something we've inherited.

Taking over requires different leadership skills than starting something from scratch. A different challenge requires a different leadership approach.

# 1

=

# INHERITING INFLUENCE

I REMEMBER IT LIKE IT WAS YESTERDAY. THE KEYS WERE HANDED TO ME. NOT to a car but to a movement. An incredibly important and beloved movement: Catalyst.

I was driving to the office for the first time in my leadership role. It was weird. I had been in my role with North Point Ministries for the past decade. My identity had been connected to that organization for years. Not only was I about to start something completely new, but my identity was also about to change. Again.

I had been with Catalyst for a year, but now I was taking the reins. The way leaders related to me was going to change. My new role involved a different set of responsibilities and greater authority. That realization elicited a fresh set of fears and insecurities but also excitement.

I remember being nervous and wondering whether I had what it was going to take to lead the organization into the future. I was curious whether I would be able to gain influence with and trust from the team that already existed and that had been investing in the organization for years.

Then I walked into the room, and I was in charge.

I had personally experienced meaningful God encounters through the movement. I had heard hundreds of leaders (I'm not exaggerating) talk about how it had changed their lives. Their families. Their churches. Their businesses.

God had handed me this movement to lead. I held the keys to Catalyst.

Catalyst had been around for fourteen years. It was a massive movement of Christian leaders that had had an impact on hundreds of thousands of leaders. It was a platform that helped catapult many artists and speakers to new heights. It had influence in the church and outside the church. With that influence came attention. Everyone had an opinion on what Catalyst should be. Everyone would have thoughts on how I should lead it.

John Maxwell. Andy Stanley. Craig Groeschel. Christine Caine. So many legends had been part of this.

My heart and mind were filled with a complete range of emotions. My spirit was overwhelmed. My joy was real; my fear might've been even more real. How in the world was I to take this *precious* (said almost like Gollum in *The Lord of the Rings*) gift and steward it to the best of my ability? What was going to be my role in its story? How was I to make changes appropriately?

I was inheriting a very special gift. I was following directors like Gabe Lyons, Jeff Shinabarger, and Brad Lomenick. These guys had led incredibly well for their seasons. How was I to follow that? Was I to try to do what they did or do something else? Was my leadership going to be up to the task?

Catalyst really matters! It wasn't like the time when I was handed the G. I. Joe aircraft carrier as a kid. Then I felt responsibility for taking care of a special toy, but how well I did so was not going to affect anyone's life. This movement had had *eternal* impact because the leaders were faith leaders. Was I ready for this?

If you're reading this book, I have a hunch that you have taken over for someone, you've been handed something, or you have a multitude of somethings and someones you're trying to lead in a God-honoring way.

You may be asking some questions, such as these that were running through my mind and heart when I inherited Catalyst:

> *What in the world is God up to?*
> *Do I have what it takes?*
> *Do I really want to take over something so loved by*
> *    so many?*
> *Is there a secret sauce to doing what the leaders be-*
> *    fore me did?*

*What if it doesn't grow?*
*Why am I scared?*
*Why am I excited?*
*Do I have to make sure I always dress cool?*
*How in the world do I get the current team on board*
*with my leadership?*
*Is everyone on the current team in the right seat on*
*the bus?*
*Are they all supposed to be on this bus?*
*What do I do if I don't like how some things are done?*
*How do I honor the past without being crippled*
*by it?*
*What if they don't think I'm as funny as I think I am?*
*How do I lead with confidence and authenticity?*
*What are others going to think about me and the de-*
*cisions I make?*
*What happens if I mess this up?*
*What happens if I succeed?*
*How do I steward the legacy of the leaders who*
*started this movement?*
*God, are You sure it's me?*

These questions were just the tip of the iceberg.

What's your experience? Have you ever been handed the keys and asked to lead something you were inheriting? Is that happening to you now? Maybe it's as simple as a job someone else did. Maybe it's a team of only two who reported to a prior leader. Maybe you are receiving someone else's vision. Or a church your parents started. Or an unfulfilled dream of the one handing it to you.

All I knew at Catalyst, with those keys in my hand, was that leading something you *start* is drastically different from leading something you *inherit*. It just is.

I'll be more specific. What are some of the differences between leading things you started yourself and leading things you didn't start? I admit this list isn't exhaustive, but here are some thoughts.

———

| NEW | INHERITED |
|---|---|
| You decide how it looks. | Someone else decided how it looks. |
| You create the expectations. | You receive spoken and unspoken expectations. |
| You choose the people. | |
| No one has decided whether you're doing a good job. | Someone else recruited the team. |
| Fear is more from the unknown. | Some people love what you do and some don't. |
| You create the culture and DNA. | Fear is more from the known. |
| You're neither profitable nor upside down yet. | Someone else created the culture and DNA. |
| You decide your location. | You're already profitable or you're upside down. |
| Expectations are forming and can't be compared with past ones. | The location is already decided. |
| | Expectations are clear and have historical backing. |
| You are new and can't be compared with the "old leaders." | You are compared with others and critiqued. |

This list could be expanded to fill an entire book. I suggest that you add or subtract items and make it your own. This might be the best exercise you could do as you begin to navigate a complex yet incredible journey.

Maybe you're taking over for someone who leads at the highest level. Or maybe you've inherited a failure that forced the past leader out. Either way, you've got some serious leading ahead. Issues like . . .

Where do you start?
Whom can you trust to talk to?
How long before making changes?

These and many other questions are why this book was written. In my twenty years working in movements started by other leaders, I've studied and focused on how to be life giving while leading something I didn't start. Actually, I believe the majority of leaders will never start something on their own but will inherit something from someone else. Things like . . .

> A job description
> A stereotype
> A space
> A church
> Relationships
> Finances
> Influence

Whoa, that last one by itself is a mind bender. How in the world do you manage someone else's influence that you are now entrusted with?

How to lead well in an inherited position might be one of the bigger issues organizations face. And it's a two-faceted challenge: What do you do when you take over something? And how do you as a leader set up your team and organization for future transitions?

So many churches today don't have succession plans. The founders have never thought through what's next. Have you ever worked for an organization where the leader didn't think anyone could do the job as well as she could? For one thing, that's not the most life-giving place to work. And it's going to be difficult for that organization to ever transition to a new leader.

As leaders, let's be wise. Let's do this right! Let's trust the timeless principles in Scripture to guide our day-to-day living and to help us navigate this potentially difficult opportunity.

One last caveat. I'm a Christian. I'm a pastor. I love to talk about how faith and life collide, how leadership is a higher calling. There are eternal consequences for how we handle the influence that's been handed to us. That's why I won't skirt around the spiritual element in leadership. For twenty-five years, my Christian faith has been the foundation of my leadership.

If you don't consider yourself a person of faith, I am still confident that this book will help you as you lead. I also think you might find here some ideas that can change the world. These concepts have stood the test of time and are called the fruit of the Spirit. They are love, joy, peace, patience, kindness, goodness, faithfulness, gentleness, and self-control.[1] These qualities will benefit any leader. But perhaps they are even more helpful for those who have inherited their leadership.

At the end of each chapter in sections 1–4, I'm going to ask you two questions to consider before moving on. Answer them honestly so that you have a good grasp of where you are in this process or where the group you've inherited is.

## QUICK QUESTIONS

1. What's one unique element of the situation you're stepping into?

2. What do you think will be most important for you starting out?

# 2

## Good Fruit

*You will recognize them by their fruits. . . . Every healthy
tree bears good fruit.*
—Matthew 7:16–17

The Peach State. I've spent the majority of my life in Georgia. When I was growing up, my family used to go to a little lake house. The groves of peach trees would always mark when we were getting closer to the vacation spot. The peach trees looked so simple—nothing great about them. Basic. Small. Nothing special.

Except.

Those basic, simple, unexciting trees produce one of the best-tasting fruits in the world. When you take a bite of a Georgia peach, you think you've gone to heaven.

Simple. Sweet. Pure. Delicious.

I'm not sure you'd ever define leadership with those words. However, anyone who has led for any length of time and led well through a unique situation will understand the sweetness of some special, satisfying moments.

Many who've never led or seen a team or organization managed in a way that actually brought life to those involved—versus taking life away—would not understand such tasty leadership fruit. Instead of simple and pure, they might think something flashy is the way to go. Maybe a charismatic leader who can be bold, brash, and fiery. Or maybe a leader who comes in with guns blazing.

I don't think the plan should be flash and bullets. That's not a good strategy. Instead, I vote to keep it simple. Start simple. Stay simple. You can't win the game on the big play if you haven't put everyone in the right position to know the play and execute it correctly. Your start as an inheriting leader is not the time for a desperate Hail Mary heave.

## BLOCKING AND TACKLING

In the South, college football is just about everyone's Saturday religion. The pageantry, energy, and "crazy" created by college football are beautiful and weird all at the same time. From an early age, kids are guided by parents as to which teams they will pull for. If the kids choose different teams when they grow up, that decision quite often feels like the story of the prodigal son! They went to a faraway place and ended up eating pig rations.

That background is necessary to understand my love for the Georgia Bulldogs. I have never played one minute of tackle football, but I've watched it my whole life, and I see some parallels to leadership. Successful football teams tend to be the best at all phases of the game. Offense, defense, and special teams. The coaches spend hours with their players in the instruction and practice of simple concepts that create the foundation for excellent performance in each of those phases. A team won't have success on offense if the offensive line can't block to protect the quarterback.

Here's what's true, though. These simple foundational skills don't ever make it as highlights on ESPN's *SportsCenter*. Some guard's clean block never makes the top ten plays featured. Instead, it's the crazy catch, the big run, or the amazing tackle for loss.

We don't hear much about the center holding his block so the quarterback stays upright long enough to complete the pass. The receiver has to run his route right to be where he should be so he can catch the ball. Everyone has to do the basics well. Without the basics, we have nothing.

Without oil, the engine won't work.

Without chairs, you can't have a service.

Without lights, it's tough to create art and mood.

You get it. The basics. As a leader, you have to fight to master the basics in order to create the great. The special. The unique. The beautiful.

## THE BASICS

If you and I were having a meal together right now, discussing what allows a leader who didn't start something to come in and be successful, I think it would be fairly easy to create a solid list of the basics:

Creativity
Patience
Flexibility
Listening
Care

That's just to name a few. Simple, right?

There's another list found in the New Testament that also seems so crazy simple. Yet I think we can agree that if most leaders would put even a couple of them into practice consistently, they would be considered amazing leaders. Here's the list, found in Galatians 5:22–23:

Love
Joy
Peace
Patience
Kindness
Goodness
Faithfulness
Gentleness
Self-Control

Nine attributes. Nine ideas.
Nine fruits.

Fruits that characterize something healthy. Helpful. Fruits that change everyone on the team for the better and that taste so good when experienced.

As I write this chapter, I'm visiting Thailand because I have the privilege of working with Compassion International to get pastors involved with child sponsorship. Thailand is just one of the many extraordinary places I've been able to visit while working with this great organization. While in Thailand, I've eaten some of the most incredible fresh fruit; some varieties I'd never seen before. They all are beautiful, delicate, and consistently delicious. Mangoes. Cherries. Rambutan, with its crazy texture and bright color. Pineapple and papaya. Maybe my favorite is the exquisite and savory dragon fruit. The texture is a little strange, but the flavor more than makes up for that! These fruits brim with healthy goodness, bringing life to those who partake of them and experience what they were designed to be. Isn't there something that makes your body instantly feel better when you eat something so fresh and tasty? Especially knowing it's really good for you! The same can be true of a leader who has good fruit to share.

Leaders who display the fruit listed in Galatians have a strong foundation for inheriting influence. When you or I join an organization or take a position where we will lead something we didn't start, we will be in a great starting place if we have equipped ourselves with these nine simple character qualities.

If you aren't quite buying this fruit thing yet, let me see whether I can convince you. And, at the risk of repeating what many incredible authors have said about the fruit of the Spirit, my goal is to show this fruit through the lens of leadership—specifically, leading in an inherited space. Much like the delicious and enriching goodness of apples, strawberries, blueberries, and watermelon (and especially peaches!), these nine qualities will make inherited leadership flourish.

One more simple side note: If, as a leader, you work and even fight to become known as one who has these qualities—this fruit—everyone will benefit. Your friends. Your organization. Your family. All of them will grow stronger, and you will see incredible growth and influence from your leadership.

## THE FRUIT

This would be a good time for a confession: When I was a kid, I rarely ate fruit. And to be honest, I still don't consume enough. It's not the taste; it's the texture. The physical structure of food has always been a tricky challenge of my diet. If it has a weird texture, I'm not sure I'm into it. Most fruits have delicious flavor, but growing up, I couldn't get past the texture. I mean, I still struggle to eat a banana! The texture of bananas and other fruits makes me nervous, even when I know that the amazing taste and nutrition are so worth pushing past the weirdness!

Okay, back to our topic . . .

As you read this book, I want you to keep the fruit of the Spirit in mind as we discuss every principle and practice that concerns inheriting influence. For example . . .

> *Where does gentleness play a role?*
> *How can peace enter the equation?*
> *Am I really required to show kindness when making*
> *a hard decision?*

Before we dive more deeply into a variety of topics, let's take a quick look at these tasty leadership fruits.

## Love

*Tyler! Really? Are you serious? I thought this was a leadership book, even a business book. We are supposed to love?*

Yeah. That's right.

Loving the team well equals leading well.

Is this taught at Harvard Business School? No.

Honestly, most business schools are committed to head-down, practical knowledge. It's not wrong; it just is what it is. But there's a reason so many leaders say they'd rather have a new boss than a pay increase.[1]

Here's the truth: if you feel loved (or cared for) by those who lead you, you'll give everything to them. And the opposite is true as well: if you don't feel like those you work with care about you, it's really hard to stay motivated.

All leaders, listen up: This fruit is not just a trendy soft people skill for your toolbox. This is a *nonnegotiable requirement.* Of course, this does not replace competency. Obviously, you can't run a marketing company on love alone. But you should wisely base your leadership on love and combine it with outstanding care for your people. When your team feel like you actually care about them, they will care for you and for the job they do. It's amazing how that works! Care will be a huge part of our plan for winning big in these situations. As you will see, care is one of the four parts of the process of leading things you didn't start. It's simply based on loving people well. Everything will depend on it. Even when you have to make hard people decisions.

I've always said that leadership is pretty simple. *Take care of those entrusted to you.*

Love and care are important in any life-giving leadership position, but they are exponentially more important when you're stepping into an inherited space. If you begin with letting those who've been there see that you are for them and will love them well, holy smokes! You will be off to a great start!

## Joy

In high school, I gave my life to Jesus and haven't looked back. If you're reading this book and you can't see how faith relates to leadership, let me tell you that this fruit is the one that changed everything for me—a true game changer. For the past twenty-five years of my life and ministry, I've made this comment over and over: *One of the characteristics that can separate Christians from those who don't believe in Jesus is joy. Joy in all things.*

I am not saying you can't have joy if you don't follow Jesus. I am saying joy is a character trait of those who do follow Jesus. He brings light in dark times, hope in the valleys of life. Good times, bad times—all of it can be joyful.

Let's do an exercise. I want you to think of someone who is full of joy. How do you know this about him? What's attractive about his life and leadership? I think the reason leaders who love and lead with joy stand out in a crowd is that this kind of leadership isn't common!

Jesus explained to His followers how living as believers, with the Spirit leading, is not easy: "The gate is narrow and the way is hard that leads to life, and those who find it are few."[2]

It may be hard and different, but it's a better life. Who doesn't want to be around leaders who bring joy and love to a team? You may be taking over something that has a toxic culture. Think for a second. You can surely see how bringing a little love and joy to a formerly toxic place would give you instant credibility.

Joy makes everything better. If you don't believe me, just give it a try for a month!

## Peace

This is a challenging fruit for me because I struggle emotionally during times of financial insecurity. Big time. For a long time. Peace is one of the last fruits to show up for me if cash is short, the bottom line is deep red, or both. I do not do well with financial struggles.

I can even have faith that God is on the move and things are looking up, but peace in my heart is hard to come by. I wish this weren't true, but it is more often than not. I've been working on this personal weakness for years, including through some therapy. Even after I've prayed through a tough financial situation and seen God show up and bring me peace, when the next crisis hits, the anxiety rises.

This is what I try to remember: we are human flesh and blood. If we count on ourselves only, ultimately we will sell our teams short. Scripture makes it clear that, for believers, the same Spirit that raised Jesus from the dead is living in us. *What?* Yes! Talk about a game changer!

So, we don't have to whip up some peace or joy?

No.

We don't have to fake it till we make it?

No.

We don't have to just pull ourselves up by our bootstraps and tough it out?

No.

Reflect on this amazing passage in Romans:

> If God himself has taken up residence in your life, you can hardly be thinking more of yourself than of him. Anyone, of course, who has not welcomed this invisible but clearly

present God, the Spirit of Christ, won't know what we're talking about. But for you who welcome him, in whom he dwells—even though you still experience all the limitations of sin—you yourself experience life on God's terms. It stands to reason, doesn't it, that if the alive-and-present God who raised Jesus from the dead moves into your life, he'll do the same thing in you that he did in Jesus, bringing you alive to himself? When God lives and breathes in you (and he does, as surely as he did in Jesus), you are delivered from that dead life. With his Spirit living in you, your body will be as alive as Christ's!

So don't you see that we don't owe this old do-it-yourself life one red cent. There's nothing in it for us, nothing at all. The best thing to do is give it a decent burial and get on with your new life. God's Spirit beckons. There are things to do and places to go![3]

For those of us who struggle with peace because we try to conjure it up ourselves, let's reread this sentence: "We don't owe this old do-it-yourself life one red cent."

Before any of us move into a new leadership space, let's give this old life a decent burial and give God a chance to fill us with His peace! Who has time for worry? Jesus gave us victory! There are things to do and people to lead!

Would you not love it if your boss led from a place of peace? Imagine a workplace or church filled with leaders at peace. I'd say that would be one great place! Now imagine yourself joining an existing team, church, or other organization and leading from an inner peace. How huge an asset would that be to your leadership?

Think about how peace would make not only your work but also your marriage, parenting, and friendships a million times more fulfilling!

## Kindness

Because I've received so much of it, kindness is the one fruit of the Spirit that has always stuck with me.

Think about it for a second. Can you remember the last time someone was kind to you? How quickly can you recall what she did? Recently, a new friend told me how excited he was about my new leadership coaching and consulting business. He wasn't just giving me lip service either, since he decided to help me get the business going by serving some of my longtime friends with gifts to say thank you for their support. He actually spent his own capital creating and sending incredible gifts to my people. Not his. It was such a generous act. I'll never forget his kindness and support!

Isn't it true that we never forget the kindness of others? Even if there are days when you might have to show them grace for a mistake or hurtful comment, you can forgive and forget with ease because the memory of their kindness has stuck with you.

Kindness is such a powerful fruit that you can use as a tool to overcome any difficult circumstances you'll face. What if you're entering a difficult place? Maybe that's why you were brought in. Maybe there was a moral failure among the leadership, or the culture was toxic, or there are financial problems or people difficulties. What if you handle the hard situations and people with kindness? It effectively cuts through the drama and office politics. Kindness yields wisdom and discernment. You build influence from day one when you are kind.

I have fought extremely hard throughout my career to be kind to everyone on my team, even when someone was let go. I know I haven't done it right every time, but I sure try. My intention when moving team members on is that they leave as friends, not enemies, of the organization. No way will they end up championing us if we aren't kind in how we handle the parting.

## Goodness

Goodness and kindness sound similar, but they actually are different qualities. I've always seen goodness as the heart condition that wants the best for the people around you.

Let's ask this: When there's someone you don't fit with or agree with deep down, do you truly want the best for her? Or do bitterness and frustration dictate your feelings toward her? Goodness comes from a place of rest. It comes from comfort in your identity. It comes from another fruit: peace.

Not every person has a ton of discernment. Actually, many struggle to understand a situation or read the actions of others. However, most of us can detect when someone is doing something with impure motives. You can tell when you're being manipulated or tricked. You can feel when someone is doing something with false pretense and dishonorable intentions.

So how do you think an existing team will feel if they know you are doing and saying nice things just because you're trying to get them to like you?

This is why these nine qualities are fruits of the Spirit. We know that, in our own strength, it's almost impossible to respond in ways that are pure and good. If you aren't connected in your spirit to the Spirit, you will have a difficult time displaying these critical fruits. Who doesn't want to work for leaders, new or old, who approach situations with goodness in their hearts? Are you picking up on the pattern developing here?

## Faithfulness

Fidelity. Constancy. Loyalty. Dependability. Trustworthiness. These all equal faithfulness.

Is there a fruit that has more layers than this one? Think about it. You can't do only one thing to be labeled faithful. You can't act a certain way one time and be considered faithful. You can, however, decide to display this trait from the time you step into your new role, knowing that it will take time for you to be proved faithful.

With something that takes time to develop, should we even worry about it from the beginning? One hundred percent yes! There are so many life principles that can prove this point, but anything worth doing takes time and requires you to start on the right path and head toward the right target. If you start off on the wrong foot, it will take longer to build trust.

I know all this fruit discussion is a lot to take in, and I'm not saying I think you can display all of them . . . Wait! We've already talked about this. You can't display all of them. Actually, you can't display any of them indefinitely! But God can. These are His fruits. Your job is to stay connected to Him. We will talk at length about this in chapter 7.

# Gentleness

I remember it like it was yesterday. I was leaving my internship at the Wesley Foundation. My mentor and pastor, Tom Tanner, took me to lunch to give me some end-of-season feedback: "Tyler, you're a great leader. It's been an honor to serve God with you. I can't wait to see what God does. Oh, and one more thing. You need to figure out your relationship with Carrie. You've got to do better. You can do better."

Gulp. This was the Carrie who later would become my wife!

I know I put what Tom said in quotes, as if I'm remembering this perfectly, but I'm sure it was something like that. All I know is that one of the men whom I respected most was telling me a hard truth. But I never would've heard that truth if he hadn't put it before me with gentleness.

If there's a fruit we all need all the time, I nominate gentleness, which requires calm, patience, emotional intelligence, and other attributes. We need the leading of the Spirit if we hope to display gentleness well.

If you have stepped into something you didn't start and choose to operate out of power and control instead of gentleness, your tenure will be short. Even when you need to make hard decisions, release a staff member, or make deep changes to an organization's culture, please do so with gentleness. Pray for God's grace in building your empathy. Say things with grace.

I think many leaders believe that if they are gentle with others on the team, especially when making tough decisions, they will be seen as weak. It's quite the opposite: You're weak when you're a jerk. You're weak when you don't tell the whole truth. You're weak when you have to make a hard decision and you handle it like a dictator with no feelings.

Tell the truth, but be gentle.

When you start to pursue changes in your inherited space, if you haven't leaned into the fruit of gentleness, you're going to have a hard time moving the team in a new direction.

# Self-Control

Sweet tea. Coke. Fried chicken. Sugar. Sugar. Sugar.

If you put any of these in front of me right now, no matter what diet or food scenario I'm working through, I'm probably going to cave. I'll talk myself into why I deserve these things.

I'm going to shoot straight with you about my personality. If this rings a bell with you, maybe we have something special in common. I can justify eating a treat any time of the day and any day of the week. The worst time for me is when I'm doing well with a plan of eating healthily. That's when I can talk myself into a treat with ease because *I've earned it.* I turn into a nine-year-old!

If there's one fruit I long to possess, it's self-control. Not because I actually want to sacrifice for this fruit but because it's the product of serious virtue and discipline.

Discipline? For me? *No thanks.*

Who likes discipline anyway? I know my nine- and twelve-year-olds don't. It can be the simplest thing, like asking them to go to bed. Based on their response, you would think I was tearing off their toenails while destroying their Lego sets and burning their Xbox.

Does your inner nine-year-old ever do that with self-control and dis-cipline? Do you ever feel like you know what's best for you—and even right—but you fight against it with every fiber of your being? Yeah. Me too.

How does this fruit play out in leading things you didn't start?

> Staying connected to God so you handle
> situations well and don't say something
> stupid
> Avoiding knee-jerk decisions
> Fighting against pushing too fast
> And an infinite number of other ways that will
> prevent you from diluting your influence

Self-control: a beautiful thing.

## Patience

You may be someone who won a badge for Sunday school attendance and learned a song or two about the fruit of the Spirit. As I've been going through this list, you caught me—I skipped patience, which usually is fourth on the list. Love, joy, peace, patience . . .

Well, in this conversation, I think patience actually may need to be number one on the list when you're inheriting a team, platform, business, or job. I think it's so important that I'm going to go into great detail and give patience an entire section of its own. Stand by!

## STARTING POINT

This is where we must start because healthy trees bear good fruit. Unhealthy trees bear bad fruit. Let's begin this inherited adventure by taking healthy fruit with us. We have to lead the way.

Are you stepping into a complete mess? Take good fruit.

Have you inherited a role from a leader who was beloved? Take good fruit.

*You* are responsible for *you*. Not what's gone before. If you want to know where to start, show the fruit.

I remember having a conversation with a close friend about this book. When I told him I believed I could base the whole book on the fruit of the Spirit, he asked, "Is that too simple?"

The truth is that often, as leaders or content creators, we feel the need to add more words, complexities, or principles. *Which I'm about to do!* However, it's important to start here, with the amazing, time-tested, God-originated fruit of the Spirit.

Let's build on a foundation that has eternal implications. Get in step with the Spirit, and hold on as we build something great in an inherited space. We can do this with God's help!

## QUICK QUESTIONS

**1.** Which fruit do you feel is lacking in your life right now?

**2.** Which fruit is going to help you gain influence with your new team?

# 3

## THE NEW KID ON THE BLOCK

*Your time is limited, so don't waste it living someone else's life.*

—STEVE JOBS

MIDDLE SCHOOL IS BRUTAL. FOR ALMOST EVERYONE. IT'S EVEN MORE DIFFIcult when you don't know anyone because you've changed schools during the summer. There's something about a change in surroundings that makes you do things that are a little crazy. Like rethinking your wardrobe or how you wear your hair. Maybe it's the way you talk or the music you listen to. For me, it was all of the above the summer before middle school. I remember thinking that, at my new school, they would know only the new Tyler. The grown-up middle-school Tyler. He was going to be a *legend.* The new weapons of my evolving identity were as follows:

> Sun In for my hair to bleach it yellow (except it
> turned red)
> A sweet Puma neon-green-and-blue bag that was
> *way* too big for a backpack
> Button-down short-sleeve shirts with all sorts of
> designs
> A gold chain
> Pleated khakis tight rolled to highlight my socks
> that matched my shirt

To finalize this look, which was a virtual guarantee that girls would like me, I wore my brand-new Bass loafers with the little swirly laces.

Are you feeling this?

## Top Notch

Prior to sixth grade, my nickname was Tyler the Smiler because all I ever did was smile and not talk. I was shy as could be. Not anymore. Arriving at the new middle school, I determined to step into my extro-version. And, boy, did I ever. My first week, three conduct-deficient documents were sent home, telling Mom and Dad I was talking too much and being sarcastic.

New school. New grade. New me. Why?

I was the new kid on the block. I wanted to fit in. I wanted to make a statement. I wanted to start strong and make friends. I wanted to be noticed and be cool.

I know that this was a sixth-grade version of me, but sometimes it's not that far from my current reality—especially when I'm the new person on the team or at the organization.

Do you ever feel that way or act like this? Just me?

I bet it's not just me. As a matter of fact, I've led teams and organizations for years now, and almost all the people I've had the privilege to lead have gone through some version of this scenario in an attempt to be different and portray themselves in a new light.

Let me make one thing clear: I'm always a fan of making yourself better. Sometimes a new start allows you to make an adjustment. A shift. Become a better version of you. However, when it comes to in-heriting influence, I really hope and pray that you've learned to lead from your truest self. That you have embraced your unique wiring and personality. We need to accept the skill of the One who designed us. (If you are questioning this, I urge you to read Psalm 139.)

In *The Life-Giving Leader,* I went deeply into the principle that strong, life-giving leaders are *okay* with whom they were uniquely made to be, which allows them to lead to the fullest. The remainder of this chapter will help you apply this principle.

## WHY YOU AND NOT SOMEONE ELSE?

My first two years of leading Catalyst were some of the most interesting and tough years of my career. Traveling frequently, I represented the movement and brand all over the country by visiting churches and businesses, explaining what we were about and where we were headed. It was an incredibly important job that I took very seriously.

However, there was this one little pattern I had developed that was subtly undermining my efforts. This pattern had been part of my life for so long that I can't remember a time when I wasn't using it as a defense against insecurity. Maybe you, too, use this behavior to deal with insecurity.

Ready for it? Drumroll . . .

*Self-deprecation.* Humor. My go-to response to all things uncomfortable.

Let me give one side note about this before we dive deep. Humor is awesome. It's one of life's greatest gifts. It can lift spirits. It can take relationships deeper. It can make you simply feel better. *When used correctly.*

As I made all those early presentations for Catalyst, though, I was using self-deprecation as a way of disguising my fear and insecurity. Humor was a way to try to hide that I felt inadequate and fearful in the job I had inherited. I would tell jokes mocking my lack of pedigree. I would laugh about having very little business experience (although I had years of planning budgets, P&Ls, and other practices). I would question why God had put me in the seat, and one time I said that God must have a sense of humor if He'd called me to this leadership opportunity.

Are you sensing the tension and awkwardness my audiences felt from these attempts at humor? I know we all laughed, probably more because I created an uncomfortable situation than because I said something really funny.

Between God's whispers and my close friends pushing, eventually I was able to see the problem. The cloud was removed, revealing what I was actually doing—*dishonoring* God's call and assignment for me. There's zero chance I was trying to do that. I needed an ointment because I was laughing at God's appointment! The medicine I needed was proper perspective.

Whether I was trying to or not, I was mocking His positioning of me.

---

When we mock the position,
we might forfeit the ignition.

---

Leaders must realize that when we are put in positions we don't understand, God can use them to launch us into the next season.

So, I had to stop the self-deprecation. To stop making fun of God's positioning and accept His good plans.

His plans to prosper me even when I'm fearful.
His plans to grow me even when I mess up.
His plans to work through me and not in spite of
me.
His plans to teach me something now so I know I
have to be dependent on Him as I lead.
His plans to reach others because of wiring He
gave only me.

There it is. The point of this entire diatribe. *You.*
Only you have been handed the reins.
The team.
The job.
The platform.
The jacked-up scenario someone left.
The church with debt and moral failure.
The church that's losing a beloved founder who's retiring.
The wildly successful business in need of new ideas.
The national spotlight.
The zero spotlight.
Whatever it is, now it's yours. And you have a choice.

## THE PATH OF LEAST RESISTANCE

This is where this chapter gets interesting and crazy practical. When God gives you an inherited opportunity, you have a choice about how you will take it. I see it going two ways:

---

• Act like the person who led it before you.
• Respect the person before you, but lead from your truest self.

---

Two options. Literally.

The first option isn't sustainable and won't bring a win for you or the organization. The people hiring you might say they want you to lead like the former leader, but I'm telling you that's not a solution worth pursuing. You aren't that former leader and never will be.

I remember once telling a holdover on a team I'd inherited, "I'm never going to be the leader I'm replacing. I'm going to be me. If that doesn't work for you, then this might not be a great fit long term."

Did that mean I wasn't focused on what the leader before me did well? Absolutely not! I saw the previous leader as a mentor, an example of how I could lead the organization. But I was also focused on what my unique strengths brought to the table. In other words, how could I multiply by addition and not divide by subtraction?

Here's a formula I've come up with for why being yourself matters in this situation:

PAST LEADER'S EXPERIENCE/GIFTING +
YOUR STRENGTHS =
*Significantly Improved Organization*

The other option is as follows:

PAST LEADER'S EXPERIENCE/GIFTING +
YOU TRYING TO BE THAT PERSON =
*Diluted Leadership Opportunity*

You haven't been handed leadership to try to be someone you're not. If you were handed it for that reason, that was poor leadership on the part of those who hired you. And it's not going to work. You will start behind. You will always lead weakly on your heels instead of leading on your toes, leaning in with strength and confidence.

The leadership potential of a well-executed transition is exponential. Making minor or major changes that align with who you are while at the same time honoring the history that built the organization can spark significant growth. At the risk of repeating the main message of *The Life-Giving Leader,* the best version of your leadership has your truest self at the center. Psalm 139 reminds us that we were knit together in our mothers' wombs for a unique story. A unique purpose.

When you are designed to lead in a certain way and choose to chase another's uniqueness, the organization is going to get a small portion of what it could and should get. That's *you. You* were picked for the job. *You* are being handed the platform. *You* were hired, not someone else.

Okay, I admit that it's tempting to try to look, act, sound, and lead like the person you're replacing. It really is. We must fight the urge to do that. We must let his leadership decisions mentor us for a season.

Let me offer an analogy. Let's say there's an Olympic track-and-field team that competes in the 4x100-meter relay. One of the team members has decided it's time to hang up the spikes, so a replacement is needed.

First, let's suppose you are interested in joining this team but your sport is golf. You wouldn't even be considered. You're a golfer. Track and field isn't your life. It's not the center point of your training. For you, running consists of occasional sprints from the course to the clubhouse because of rain. In other words, you wouldn't be considered for the relay team because you don't have the required competency. Having the fundamentals is absolutely nonnegotiable.

Second, even if you were a runner, you would have to stand out to be picked over all the other runners who've made their careers sprinting. You would have to show that *you* have something the team needs. Something that would make the team better simply because you were added.

Lastly (and maybe this is the hardest part), let's say you were chosen and are going to fill the spot of someone who's been a rock—maybe even the anchor—for this team for a long time. This person is loved. Respected. Family. What's the instant temptation? To try to be that person! Run like she did. Communicate like she did. Basically, be the best version of her that *you* can be. Do you see the problem? There's only one her. And there's only one you.

I know I'm repeating myself a little, but stay with me. Would it be a good idea to watch film and learn how the runner you're replacing best helped the team? Of course! That's called being professional. Due diligence. Training.

But. And this is a big *but.* Learn from her, but do not try to be her. You're fresh. You've got unique skills and style. You bring something to the team that they've never had before. Again, you wouldn't have been selected if your basic skills and talents were in question. You were selected *because* of those skills and talents. Rest in that.

Learn from the person you're replacing. But be *you.*

## THE OTHER SIDE OF THE COIN

Why don't we take a minute and look at this from the other side? I remember my friend Clay Scroggins sharing an illustration about why golfers walk around on the green before they line up and putt. He shared the importance of seeing the hole from the other side. You might *feel* like the putt's downhill until you walk around and realize it's ever so slightly uphill. You never would've seen it without a different perspective.

What if you were the hiring manager and one of your best employees left? He was offered a new opportunity, and it made sense for him to jump at it. You have to replace a great player—someone who was loved and brought massive talent to the table. Have you ever thought about someone on your team, *I'm not sure what I'd do if he walked out the door?* That's the kind of person I'm talking about. How would you even start to replace him? What would you look for?

Here are several questions I like to ask myself when this happens:

> *What did the former employee do in this role that*
> *has to be part of the new employee's skill set?*

>	*What intangibles did the person bring to the team*
>	    *that I'd like to look for?*
>	*Does this iteration of the position even look the*
>	    *same as it did before? Has the organization*
>	    *changed, requiring this position to change with a*
>	    *rehire?*

Then stop and consider this: *You are never replacing a person. You are hiring a new position.* We have to understand this as leaders. *People aren't replaceable.* How someone does something is her trademark. It's her likeness, who she is. Are there fundamental skills needed for the position? Yep. But is how the position done up for conversation? It had better be.

Good luck replacing someone. It takes a ton of pressure off us as leaders when we realize we don't have to do that. Instead, we have to lead. We have to look at all the factors and decide which ones are the most important in this rehire.

---

Every time a team member transitions out,
it is an incredible opportunity to reset or
double down on the position.

---

I hate losing great people. I've been asked before, "Does it bother you when you invest in and get close to team members and then they leave?" One hundred percent. It absolutely crushes me. Every. Single. Time. I don't pour my life and leadership into leaders without time, heart, soul, and love. So, yes, it hurts when they leave. However, I know the double-edged sword of leadership: you invest and they become better, or you invest and they leave. I hate to break it to you, but they will leave. Always. It's just the truth. No one stays forever.

So, if you choose not to get close to your team members because they will leave, then you have a sad leadership plan. You're choosing to alienate yourself from the people you've been entrusted with. Do you have to tell them everything? All your fears, thoughts, insecurities? Nope. But you need to be willing to give your life and leadership to them. You cannot be life giving unless you *give* of yourself. That's the necessary transaction.

Why do I bring this up now?

Because there are many of us who take a very technical approach to leading people and keep that approach when hiring replacements. People are people, right? You can hire based on certain metrics, but if you never take the time to think about how to hire a new *person* and see how his skills, uniqueness, and talents play into the bigger picture, then you will struggle to find and retain great talent.

No one wants to replace a beloved team member if you seem to want your new hire to be the former employee's twin. I'm not taking that job. Would you? So you shouldn't offer that job. You want the new hire to succeed, don't you? Do your homework on the front end to make your expectations realistic for her. You want her best! Don't suffocate her with unspoken expectations related to a former team member.

## FIRST TO MARKET

I'm going to keep the end of this chapter quite simple: You, the leader, have to be first to market. If you aren't leading from your truest self, how can you expect your team to? You have to go first. Lead the way. Show them that being themselves is what you want, *especially* if they are new to your team.

Here's a little mental exercise to help you evaluate whether you are leading from your truest self. Ask yourself these questions:

> *Do I feel comfortable in my own skin?*
> *Am I acting or leading in any way that feels outside*
> *   my uniqueness?*
> *Am I fearful of anything?*
> *Is there anything in my leadership now that runs*
> *   counter to how I normally lead?*

I can't promise you much, but I can tell you that I believe and have seen that leaders who lead from this place of confidence in who they are tend to experience significant success in the spaces they inherited.

Just try it! What do you have to lose?

## QUICK QUESTIONS

1. How have I tried to lead in a way that isn't natural to me at this time?

2. How can I focus on truths about me and not buy into lies?

# Section 2

## THE IMPORTANCE OF HONORING AND LEARNING FROM THE PAST

ABOUT A YEAR AGO, I WAS HEADED TO SPEAK AT CLEMSON UNIVERSITY. Even though I'm a die-hard Georgia Bulldog, I looked forward to hanging with some students at their campus ministry.

I did a leadership talk I've done multiple times on how to be prepared to lead in the future by working on your character today, before you ever get the opportunity to lead.

I had a great time, and it was a blast being on the campus. I love college students. I digress. Anyway, on my two-hour return drive, God started speaking to me. I realized how much of my time with students had been spent on practical leadership principles and how little time was devoted to God's Word around those ideas. I'd presented a horizontal step-by-step guide but without a strong why.

What I felt God was showing me is that I have the opportunity to point people in a vertical direction before revealing to them some practical steps on leading. I have the same opportunity now—to point you to God before we talk about how to lead in an inherited situation.

Are you okay with one more moment of vulnerability? During the entire process of writing this book, I've been wrestling in my head and heart with that same conversation I had with God. I know the leadership principles, and often I'll skip some of the spiritual parts to get to the practical tools that will help others right now.

I want to ask you to do something. Whether you pray and read the Bible daily or you've never done either one, would you consider starting each chapter of this next section with a simple prayer? Would you ask God to show you what His heart is for how you should lead in your new season? Would you look up to Him with me before we look forward together?

As we continue this journey, this section will walk you through the early days of learning from the past you have inherited. What to do first. Where to start so that you will know where to go.

My belief is that the very best way to start is to pause and look up.

"I lift up my eyes to the hills. From where does my help come?"[1]

# 4

## HONORING THE PAST WITHOUT GETTING TRAPPED BY IT

*[Focus] on honoring what is most beautiful about our past and building it into the promise of our future.*
—JACQUELINE NOVOGRATZ

THE PAST. WHEW. THIS CHAPTER WILL REQUIRE SOME INTROSPECTION. SOME work. Some heavy lifting. We can't avoid the past. We must look at it. There's absolutely zero chance we can move on successfully and lead into what's next without understanding what's happened.

*Oh, wait. This is about leadership at work—not my personal past, right?* Wrong.

I've never believed you can divorce your life from your work. I'm not saying to bring all your junk to the job every day, but life happens, and it happens to you and to me. Why am I bringing this up?

This book is 100 percent about leading things you didn't start, but machines don't lead—people do. People are complicated. People have emotions. People have hopes and dreams. No matter how great a leader you are, you are still, well, *you.*

You have emotions. You have hopes and dreams. And you have a past.

Rest assured, we will get to all the implications of and principles for leading something you didn't start. However, we have to begin with this simple premise: *If you don't know you, you can't lead through.* Through the next obstacle. Through the next season. Through this transition. All these things need you. The real you.

So simple, right? Not really.

About three years ago, I had the privilege and pain of going to On-site Workshops.[1] Miles Adcox, a longtime friend, runs this incredible mental and emotional health retreat center outside Nashville. Their theme is "life-changing personal growth and emotional wellness experiences." I describe what they do as "a retreat to feel again, to see yourself correctly, and to make small adjustments that lead to big turnarounds." I went for a very specific reason—my scarcity mentality.

I've struggled with a scarcity mindset since I was young. As a family, we didn't have a lot of material things, so I basically operated from a posture that said, *If it's not in my hands, it can't be real.*

That approach served me fine for the first twenty-five to thirty years of my life. But the next decade or so, not so much. Plus—and this is a huge *plus*—I don't believe I serve a God of scarcity. In my thirties, I was getting tired of always tripping over this mentality. And it was even affecting how I led organizations. When there was financial insecurity anywhere in my life, it was crushing me. My spirit and emotions were being sautéed in fear.

Onsite was a game changer for me. It didn't fix all the realities at home or work. I didn't experience an overnight turnaround. I certainly left in a better place, but what I really gained was an understanding of where my scarcity mindset came from. Where that struggle was based and why it was still with me. I also went to Onsite because I didn't want to ingrain this belief in my two sons. I want them to believe in an *abundant* heavenly Father.

I'm still fighting for a change in behavior and emotional peace during those times when I don't see abundance. But I understand better now what triggers my emotions and insecurities, and I can address them before and during the seasons when they are being tested.

I bring this up for one reason: when I step into leading something I didn't start and there are financial pressures, I'll be prepared because I know this about myself. I'll have a leg up on the pressures and frustrations my entire team will be feeling.

Again, *you just cannot lead well without knowing yourself.* If you have never dealt with *your* past, it's going to be hard to understand how to manage the past of an organization and its leadership, to grasp how and why decisions were made.

Organizations and teams are no different than we are as individuals. Organic. Alive. Emotional. We have to understand where the group has been to understand where to take it and how. I believe that when you've done this kind of homework in your own life, it'll help you understand how to diagnose and learn from the organization's history. Plus, you'll find helpful tools for your own leadership journey by working on your self-awareness. You will never inherit influence well unless you understand and honor your personal past.

If you are convinced you can have a you at work and the real you everywhere else, you can. For a while at least. But being divided like that is really a lack of integrity, and you are at great risk of burning out as you try to be all things to all people.

I believe there are five areas that all leaders should focus on if they are to honor the past well and lead an inherited organization or team into the future with competence and strength.

## 1. CELEBRATE APPROPRIATELY

If I have convinced you of the importance of knowing your personal past, then you're ready to embrace the value of learning the past of the situation you are stepping into. If you don't take a serious look at what has gone on before you, you will not be prepared to address problems and celebrate victories.

Have you ever shown up to a meeting and realized everyone else in the room had a ton of information but you didn't? You're handcuffing yourself and your team from the start. Why would you do that to yourself? We have to fight our tails off just to enter the arena (as Steven Pressfield put it in *The War of Art*).[2] If you accept the assignment and step into the arena, you'd better do some homework to prepare yourself for what you might encounter.

Are you familiar with the Hunger Games series? As a reminder, this three-book, four-movie epic story concerns a sovereign state—Panem—that is governed by an oppressive group living in the Capitol. The leader, President Snow, operates as if the government keeps the peace and has provided life for so many, even though it's clear very early in the story that's not true.

Quickly you realize there are twelve districts in Panem. Each district is known for some resource, skill, or food. Farmers, technicians, and so on. One of the demented ways Snow likes to keep his thumb on the lives of those in the districts and continue to show how ruthless the Capitol can be is the yearly Hunger Games. All twelve districts are required to send one male and one female tribute (participant) to the games. The most brutal part of the story is that these twenty-four people are playing for their lives. Only one survivor. It's intense, to say the least.

I so clearly remember the scene where all the tributes are being trained for *whatever* they might face. On the train ride from their districts to the Capitol, they are each taught the history of the Hunger Games and how the game makers have taken out tributes in the past. Then, while they prepare and train for the actual games, they work with every weapon and learn every survival technique. They not only focus on what they are best at but also gain confidence in areas that are not their expertise. Not that they will all of a sudden crush those areas, but they will have some familiarity with them *just in case* they need it. Every aspect of their skill and mental preparation will be called on during this life-and-death sport.[3]

Now, look. Don't direct message me because the Hunger Games were life-and-death and this is just leadership. No one is dying. Well, hopefully that's true.

However, you'd better prepare as if any scenario could play out. As if you could lose the entire game within the first period because of your lack of preparation. Your lack of understanding. Your inexperience. Your fear.

It's on *you* if you don't learn the skill of honoring the past.

---

> If you don't honor what's been successful,
> you lose your ability to be influential.

---

You cannot do this without understanding the historical context you're walking into. Teams will not trust you or believe in you if you show no respect for what they've been through.

I'm serious when I say that planning and preparation absolutely wear me out. I'm crazy unstructured in life. The fact that you're reading my second leadership book is proof that God exists and fills in the gaps where we are lacking! The amount of work required for a leadership book like this is insane.

Outlines
Research
Felt needs
Audience
Writing
Word counts
Editing
Endnotes
More drafts
Proofreading

All this and more!

Is your "Hunger Games experience" inheriting a team or platform that already exists? History. Great accomplishments. Terrible decisions. Maybe moral failures. Perhaps a recent record of outstanding success.

Whether it's good or bad, you have to *honor* it. Period. If you have any desire to rally a team or make them understand that you are for them, you first have to show that you know them. Where they've come from. Where they've been hurt. Where they've crushed it. It's important to plan how you will honor the past—it can't be ad lib. Celebrate all the good publicly. This needs to be sincere. However, it might take some manufactured energy since you know all the good and the bad. But you have to do it. To gain influence, pour life into the people by celebrating them well.

## 2. HONOR THE RIGHT THINGS

You may already have jumped ahead in your mind and are frustrated at the thought of having to fake it or act as though someone did a good job when he didn't. Relax—that's not what I'm suggesting. There might

be no quicker way to lose influence with your new team than by celebrating someone who really did damage to the people who are still
there.

I've struggled with this off and on in my career. On the RightPath
assessment, I'm an encourager, so it comes relatively easy for me to be
hopeful and thankful for people. I somehow always see the good in a
person or situation, even when the majority might've been bad. I've
had to learn how to manage this quality by having staff around me
who will speak candidly to me when a team member is having a negative effect by her poor performance. Without the input of others, my
blind spot might cause me to celebrate someone whose behavior or
performance is not exemplary.

I've talked about this for years and heard this statement a million
times in my career: *Leadership isn't just what you do. It's what you allow.*

How true! This is one of the hardest parts of leadership in general,
but it's incredibly difficult when you are transitioning into a spot where
leadership was lacking. If you celebrate the wrong parts of the past,
you will potentially create a wrong impression of what you want winning to look like for the team. Does that make sense?

---

When and how you celebrate the past leaders
and successes will create a baseline for what is
going to be allowed and celebrated in the future.

---

I cannot emphasize this enough! You have to be strategic in this inheriting season. Since my spiritual gift is flying by the seat of my pants,
I had to learn to be particularly careful and wise during this time of
honoring the past.

## 3. SHIFT FOCUS

I remember my first few months after I joined the team at Catalyst. My
boss and the longtime leader of the movement, Brad Lomenick, had
given me the task of pouring myself into leading the staff by working
with and developing them. He understood that since we were an orga-

nization devoted to leadership training and development, we had to be good at it ourselves. I can remember saying this statement more than any other: *"When I'm talking about where we need to go, it's not a reflection of good or bad within the organization; it's a direction for the future."*

So often we step into existing spaces and the proposed changes are seen as negative and dishonoring of the past. I don't believe that has to be the response, but will it be if the transition isn't handled well? Of course. Hence this book needing to be written!

I believe you can make appropriate changes that aren't indictments against the past. Instead, they are new beliefs for the future, stated like this: "Where are we going, and how are we going to get there? Oh, and why is this better?"

In the last section of this book, there are interviews with leaders who've stepped into existing places and had to keep this principle central to their leadership. Coach Buzz Williams has done this four times in his career as a head collegiate men's basketball coach. Every time he's changed schools, he's stepped into an existing program with all its flaws and successes. Every time, he's been smart to honor those coaches and players who've gone before and paint a picture of where he wants the program to go. This beginning requires thought and careful implementation.

It's delicate.

It's a dance.

It's leadership.

So, in an inherited space, where should you focus? What's the starting point?

Do you remember before Instagram was crazy popular and made you believe you were a professional photographer? You used to have to own a great camera and special lenses and know how to use all that equipment to get some of the amazing effects that now are done easily with an app. It's insane! Well, there was one effect you could get from what's called a tilt-shift lens. It kept one part of the image in focus while everything else blurred. It made mundane shots gorgeous and look like Ansel Adams had decided to jump on your shoot. You didn't even have to be great at framing; you just had to know what you were looking for and put that in focus.

Something similar can happen when you inherit influence. When you step into an existing team or role, you should come prepared to tilt shift. You focus on the main objective first while also determining the organizational items that need to be set aside or temporarily "blurred out." A skilled tilt shift can be instrumental in your early success.

Let's look now at a few questions that will help you discover where the focus should be early on. Please note that, in the next couple of chapters, we will spend considerable time on the process of evaluation that will shape your plan of attack and focus your attention. However, I feel it necessary to start scanning for indicators of problems. So here are some beginning questions:

> How strong is the team? *For real.*
> What financial situation are we in?
> What fires have to be put out?
> What fears and insecurities are floating around the team?
> What essential services are missing to keep us afloat or move us forward immediately?
> How's the leadership? Board? Directors?
> Am I coming into a spot where I'm fresh air or replacing a beloved leader? (This honestly might be the simplest yet most important question to answer before you get started.)

If you can answer most of these questions before day one, you are well on your way to a strong starting baseline.

Now, I need to say something so that I'm not overlooking a huge assumption. I am aware that readers of this book are entering at different levels in their organizations. I fully understand that if you're inheriting an entire movement, church, or business, the focus will be quite different than if you're stepping into an entry-level role in a smaller place. Either way, there will be something you'll have to focus on. You'll have to see the realities you're facing. The deeper your dive before you show up, the better you can discern how you want to lead.

You may be saying, "I wish I'd had this information *before* I took this job." I think you can conduct the majority of this research during the interview process. I've talked with hundreds of leaders who expressed their frustration with not knowing all that they were inheriting. I urge you to *do your homework* as soon as possible! When you go to an interview, they are not just interviewing you; you are interviewing them. Before you agree to take the position, you have to make sure you've asked every question. I can't tell you how important this is.

The crazy part is that there is no way you can learn everything ahead of time. I'm just telling you that the more you know, the better. Even when you unearth some details that are going to be tough to lead through, it doesn't mean you shouldn't take the opportunity. It just helps you make an informed decision about the possibilities and the challenges you'll face.

## 4. Cast New Compelling Vision

I looked it up, and seven trillion books and articles have been written on the subject of vision. Okay. I might be exaggerating and didn't actually look it up, but on my shelf I have at least fifteen books on the topic. I'm not sure I'm going to add a ton of new ideas to the conversation, but I want to reframe the *why* behind this principle.

Maybe the most consistent kind of conversation I have with my wife is when she details something that happened or something she saw during her day. Many times she's been to a house or other space that she loved, and she attempts to paint a picture for me of what it looked like. Here's the crazy thing: I'm actually a visual learner—I think in pictures. But I can almost *never* understand the layout or concept she's painting without an actual picture! Are you that way? If not you, then for sure most—if not all—of the people you work with are!

If you can't see what something looks like, even with an accurate description, it's often difficult to get motivated or excited about it. This is absolutely the case when you enter an inherited situation. So many on your new team will not be able to see what you're seeing down the road. It's going to be of utmost importance that you learn the art of casting vision. In fact, not just vision but *compelling* vision! Even if it means hard work and difficult decisions.

A vision that moves people.

A vision that creates emotional buy-in.

A vision that makes them say, "Let's go!"

I love what my former boss and pastor Andy Stanley said about vision: "The greatest motivator of change is a crystal clear picture of what the future should look like."[4]

The word from Andy's statement that jumps off the page for me is *should*. Without this one little word, this seems like just another thought on vision. However, this *should* make it a world-changing thought on vision. Vision isn't just about where we *could* go or what we *could* do. What the future *might* entail. No! Compelling vision is filled with images of what we *should* do! What we are called to do! Where we are called to go! Vision should be filled with passion! Do you feel my passion with all my exclamation points?

We will do a deep dive into vision in chapter 11, but here are several quicker thoughts.

Tell the team that the ship is going to sail in a new direction, including where and why. Don't hesitate. If you don't know all the answers . . . welcome to leadership! Rally the team. Show them how the vision needs them! Show them your role in it. Paint the picture with vivid details. Dig deep. (You can see why this can't happen until you've done the first three steps in this chapter.)

Simon Sinek has one of the top five TED Talks of all time based on *why*—how a leader must explain where he wants to go.[5] You have to start with why. Your team will want you to skip over this and drill down on how the vision will affect them. Don't go there yet. Instead, focus on the *why*. Why are we giving our lives to this? Why should we pour our best into this place? This team? This vision?

Once you actually know and are confident in where you are going, you can focus on how to get there.

There's one last step in this process of honoring the past and not getting trapped by it. You have to move on.

## 5. Move on from Honoring

"Every scholar of the Scriptures, who is instructed in the ways of heaven's kingdom realm, is like a wealthy home owner with his house filled with treasures both new and old. And he knows *how* and *when* to bring them out to show others."[6]

I love this passage. The owner knows *how* and *when* to bring out the treasures, both new and old. Leaders who can move into an existing team or organization and make it better than before have an understanding of this principle. Discernment about when to move on from the past and not feel the need to honor it anymore will be crucial in your journey. I'm not saying you will switch from honoring to dishonoring. Never. It's just simply moving on. No more do we need to make sure the past gets its due. Instead, we move into the new season.

Are you wondering how long until you move on?

I have no idea. It depends on the situation. If you're stepping into a small team or you're taking over for someone but aren't leading at the top, it might be a week. If you're inheriting an entire platform, company, or church, it will be much longer. How long? Again, discerning the climate in the organization and the love the team has for the past will help you determine the length you need to honor it.

When I took over at Catalyst, I intentionally chose to honor those whose shoulders I was standing on longer than I probably had to. Honestly, I thought about them at every event for four to five *years*. That's right—years! *Way too long.* I needed to move on and lead. Often I was concerned that people were still comparing me with the past leadership. I needed to put aside my insecurity and lead. Trust the Lord. Ask some trusted leaders around you how they feel. Trust your team. Move on.

If you don't, you will be stuck. In the mud. In the history. With the old expectations. With your fears. With the old style.

Read this next paragraph carefully. It may be why you picked up this book. Ready?

---

Move on. You've honored the past and the leaders of the past long enough. Now lead. Move into the compelling vision. Give the team a picture of what they should do. You've stepped in with such grace; now lead!

---

So far we've addressed many areas that you need to consider early on in order to serve the team you've inherited. Understand their gifts. But what about the gift only you can bring to the table? You will see things no one on the existing team can see because you're new. And you have fresh eyes.

## QUICK QUESTIONS

1. What is something that clearly needs to be honored early and often?

2. What needs to disappear and not return?

# 5

===

# FRESH EYES

*Your perspective will become either your prison or your passport.*

—STEVEN FURTICK

IF YOU CAN'T TELL BY NOW, I LOVE LEADERSHIP. I LOVE ASSESSMENTS THAT make us better leaders. I love figuring out ways to grow my emotional intelligence (EQ). I mean, seriously, the coaching and evaluation of leadership is central to my operating system.

I love it, but I never said it's easy. It's hard. Especially when you're working on yourself.

That brings me to the dreaded 360 evaluation.

If you have never heard of a 360 evaluation, let me give you the thirty-thousand-foot view. The main idea is to have people who live and work all around you rate you in several key leadership areas. Raters are . . .

> Your bosses
> Your direct reports (those you lead)
> Your peers
> Your family and friends

So, up, down, and equal.

The purpose of a 360 evaluation is to get a better understanding of how people around you perceive you and your leadership. Many articles on leadership talk about blind spots or lack of self-awareness. The 360 concept is simple: Which areas do others know you struggle with but you don't?

Now, I know you probably are very self-aware, but maybe someone you work with isn't, and she needs to read this chapter (wink wink). For kicks, let's assume we all have areas of weakness in our leadership that we can't see. How in the world would we figure them out if we can't see them? A 360 evaluation might be a good start.

I'm not going to lie—it's not exactly the most fun thing you will ever do. Let me fill you in on the first time I had a 360 evaluation. I'll preface it by saying that even though my scores turned out pretty good, the pain of unearthing things about my leadership was real. Plus, when you're giving people a chance to answer anonymously, it can always be a little tricky. But it was time for me to have it done.

I had my good friend and longtime coach, Fran LaMattina, curate my assessment. She helped me land on who my raters would be, and then she administered the evaluation to each rater and gathered the information. When I got the evaluation back, although it really was quite positive, my eyes weren't drawn to the high-scoring characteristics. They were drawn to which part? Yep, my lowest. *What did my friends and leaders not like about me? What were their perceptions about me that were different from my own?* Push pause. Did you catch that?

What were their perceptions about me that were *different from* my own perceptions about my leadership?

Yoinks! Not easy, but oh so necessary! I warned you about the 360 . . .

There they were. My two lowest scores. The lowest by far was time management. Well, that's not really a blind spot. I will never be great at time management. I can get a little better, but I'll never try to fake it—to pretend like I'm great at it. That one didn't bother me or surprise me.

The second to last one did . . . one of my lowest scores. *Listening.*

"What? I didn't hear you. Can you repeat that?"

Yep. Listening.

For someone who's off-the-charts relational, this score hit me deep. But it wasn't just the score that hurt. It was particularly painful for two reasons:

1. My direct reports—*my team*—were the ones who rated me the lowest on this quality!
2. My personal perception was not that I was low in the area of listening but that being a good listener was actually one of my strengths!

Perception is reality. None of us like this, but I believe it's true.

---

What people receive is what they perceive.

---

If you're telling me one thing with your words but your body language makes me perceive something else, then my perception becomes my reality. Not what *you* think is reality. This is one of the reasons that communication is so important. Without making others' perceptions and our realities match, we will constantly struggle.

For me and my 360, the journey had just begun. I had to figure out why my self-perception was so out of whack with my team's reality. I started a deep dive into all the avenues in which my team would be in contact with me. Plus, I asked what my one-on-one meetings were like. I asked each team member questions to try to find some clarity on what I did that made them feel I wasn't so good at listening. It was a fascinating and strenuous discovery of self. Here is, to the best of my recollection, what I figured out.

I learned from my team that it wasn't in one-on-one meetings where they didn't feel heard; rather, it was in our larger meetings. Most of our meetings consisted of a combination of creative, preproduction, and evaluation. Often it was just a passing of information from me to them. Many times we jumped straight to creative brainstorming.

My brain moves quickly. Like Dash in *The Incredibles* quick. Lack of focus is natural for me. My brain moves from one idea to the next email to the last text and finally to what I want to eat at Chick-fil-A. A split second. There are some reasons for this. Throughout my time working with this team, I was forced to bounce back and forth from execution to creative to evaluation and back again within meetings. Sometimes multiple times within a meeting. I was always leading the team through these processes.

Ultimately, here's what I discovered about myself. When someone shared an idea or gave an update, my brain jumped directly to two places before he got even a quarter of the way through his communication:

1.   I know what he is going to say.
2.   Where do I need to go next in this meeting?

In almost every meeting, I was changing gears in my mind way before I had listened well to each team member. How did he know I wasn't listening? Body language—all day long.

In *The Life-Giving Leader,* I spent much-needed time talking about the power of body language and posture. If you don't believe it matters, well, you're wrong!

My team started noticing when I was done listening. I was so bummed when I realized how they had been receiving my leadership for years, yet I was excited that I could make a change and get better! One of the greatest gifts a 360 or similar evaluation gives a leader is a reality check. A fresh look at areas that have become normal, maybe even celebrated.

What the 360 did for my leadership shows what can happen when you step into an existing team with fresh eyes. You are evaluating the organization, team, or position you are inheriting! It's a gift! For years I would tell any new staff member who came to work with us the same thing: "It's a gift to us that you are here. You will have fresh eyes for only so long before they lose their ability to see. Ask us every question that comes to mind!"

*Fresh eyes give fresh perspective.*

If you don't capitalize on this gift within your team or organization, it's like dropping the Super Bowl–winning pass because you took your eyes off the ball.

Often I hear a truth or principle and I agree. The struggle is knowing how to take advantage of the insight. How do you best make use of fresh eyes? I'm glad you asked.

## Embracing Fresh Eyes

There are four actions we can take to embrace fresh eyes:

1. Create a safe space.
2. Ask new teammates what they see—be specific.
3. Let new members ask you why you do things the way you do them.
4. Be willing to see new perspectives and make changes if necessary.

Before we discuss the four actions, I need to make a comment. This chapter works for both new leaders and new team members. If you are new to a team or organization, you should evaluate whether you are in a safe place to share what you see. If you are leading an organization or team, you need to put this into practice with your current staff. Either way, taking advantage of your fresh eyes or a new teammate's perspective will be a critical tool in your tool kit. As you read about these four action steps, consider how to apply them to your situation.

## 1. Create a Safe Space

I know this sounds like an easy action, but it actually might be the hardest of all four. Let's put it in a way that might more easily hit home. Forget work for a minute. Think of someone who's in your inner circle. I'll use my wife for this example.

My wife and I have been married for eighteen years. *Cue the applause!* If there's a place that should be safest on the planet for me, it's with her in my home. Yet if I'm honest, oftentimes in that space I find myself more defensive than I am in other places in my life. I can take criticism or pushback from peers at work *way* easier than from the person closest to me. Is that not the craziest thing you've ever heard? There is no one on the planet who cares for me more and has more passion for me to succeed than she does.

And yet.

I get more defensive and put more walls up to protect myself from her input than I do from anyone else's. It doesn't make any sense. It's just truth. I know I'm not the only one.

If we know that and we know we need to create safe spaces, then why do we not do a better job of it? How do we change?

The most obvious answer is that we need to become more self-aware and change others' perception. After eighteen years of being defensive, until I invite my wife into the space and create a safe spot for her to share, I'm not sure it will change. People will give feedback only until it's clear that either the feedback is landing on deaf ears or they're not safe to deliver it.

When it comes to inheriting influence, you have to walk delicately through this action of creating a safe space. You might be entering a place that isn't safe, and you're going to have to change that. You might have to be bold and talk often about what you see. Early on, you will have to use your emotional intelligence to wade through some of these observations and present your thoughts in a way that gains trust. What's not an option? Saying nothing. You're seeing things that some of the team haven't been able to see in years! That's valuable information that the individuals and organization need to know.

## 2. Ask New Teammates What They See— Be Specific

I think it's important to always grab a few minutes with new team members during their first day or two. You have to set the tone that you are approachable and care about them as people. As a leader, you're never so high up in an organization that you can remove yourself from new staff. Never.

Create safety early. Let the new people know that you see their fresh eyes as a gift. For only a few weeks or months, these new team members, if given the space, could discover an issue or missing component that catalyzes your church or organization! They have to be asked. They have to know they can ask. They need to feel safe enough to ask why the culture is like it is.

Ask the new staff members specific questions:

"Has anything happened early on in your time
  with us that you felt was counter to what we
  said we are about?"
"What's something in our culture that makes you
  confused or uncomfortable?"

If you do this well, you will stay fresh and prevent toxic behaviors.
Now, if you are the new one, look for the leadership to let you step
into the space with questions like this. This leads to my next action
step.

## 3. Let New Members Ask You Why You Do Things the Way You Do Them

You do this already when something goes south.

I remember an amazing *Saturday Night Live* sketch that portrayed
this concept perfectly. Every time someone in the family found something that was out of whack, she'd yell to everyone else about how
jacked up it was and say, "You've gotta try this!" It was so extreme and
ridiculous. But that's what made it feel so real.

"Yuck! This milk smells terrible. You've gotta smell
  this!"
"Holy smokes—when you step on this rusty nail, it
  really hurts! Come see for yourself!"
"That noise is killing my ears! Listen!"

It was hilarious yet painful to watch because it hit so close to home.
Work is no different sometimes. We often keep doing things, even
when we know we should make changes. Why? Oftentimes it's easier
to stay with what we know, even when what we know isn't best.

I used to tell our new staff to ask any questions that came to mind
about why we did things the way we did them. If our only answer is
"Because we've always done it that way," that's not sufficient. This is a
great starting place for deep dives into what changes are needed. Listen carefully to questions like these:

"Why do team members talk about one another?"

"Why does this group not like that group?"

"What's up with the vacation policy?"

"Why does the staff manual mention a policy that clearly doesn't get implemented?"

Now, if you've always done it a certain way because you have data to show it's still the best way, then keep that train rolling. However, if changes are needed, then you have to be open to them.

## 4. Be Willing to See New Perspectives and Make Changes If Necessary

I'll never forget the staff meeting at North Point Community Church when we walked in and saw this old couch with floral upholstery sitting on the stage. We had no idea why it was there. Andy Stanley ignored it for most of the meeting, until he started his leadership talk for the day.

He talked about how an old couch can sit in your home so long that you forget it's there. Only when someone comes over who's never seen it before does it stand out like a sore thumb. It's usually an old design with old fabric, and it might even smell a little. But it has serious sentimental value, as most things do. Even within teams and organizations, products and programs that were innovative and inspiring years ago still have a place because we love them too much to cut them.

It wasn't until the end of the talk that Andy sat on the old couch and explained how his parents had a couch that looked like that and they never thought anything about it. They no longer saw it for what it was. It became normal and part of the fabric of their house. We can't *not* see these things. Allow fresh eyes to shine light on them! That's why fresh eyes are so valuable. They see differently. They see the old couch. They see the elements that have become invisible to those who've been there the longest. They see the program that's dying.

I was recently consulting with an organization that had a donor event every year. As I listened to the numbers and the plan, I quickly realized—because I had fresh perspective—that this event was draining cash. A donor event, designed to raise money, was losing it. The problem was that everyone was used to doing the event the way it had always been done. Everyone was so busy with his other work that no one raised his hand and pointed out the reality.

I saw it. I raised my hand. Without my fresh eyes, they might've gone on for years with the donor event, their version of the old couch! To their credit, as soon as I pointed out the discrepancy, they followed this key step we are talking about and made changes. They knew this problem needed to be fixed, and they jumped on it. Now they are building new events and plans to actually raise money instead of losing it. That's leadership!

## Hidden Pictures

This entire chapter reminds me of a magazine I grew up with. Anytime I was in a doctor's office, I looked for the kids' magazine *Highlights*. It was the best, mainly for one reason: the Hidden Pictures page. My brother and I would literally fight over it.

Basically, there was a picture of a nature scene or a schoolroom or something simple. Within the picture were ten or so hidden images that didn't belong. The objective was to find each hidden picture. Nothing was worse than turning to that page with heartfelt expectation and seeing that some chump kid had circled all the hidden pictures! Ugh. I still get mad thinking about it. But if the page was clean, you had to change your perspective to see what was there. Things were just hidden.

When you inherit influence and step into something you didn't start, this is a skill you'll have to develop. You must use your fresh eyes to see the hidden pictures.

Dig in. Ask great questions. Be curious.

---

Curiosity paves the way for
gaining quick influence.

---

Curiosity will help you start building your framework as you lead this new team. Now that you know you are looking for the hidden pictures, it's time to figure out just what you should be looking for.

## Quick Questions

1. Where do I need fresh eyes?

2. What do I need to be more curious about?

# 6

## EVALUATION IS BRUTAL BUT NECESSARY

*Without proper self-evaluation, failure is inevitable.*
—JOHN WOODEN

I LOVE GOLF. I MEAN, PROBABLY TOO MUCH. IT'S AN OUTLET AND MY STRESS reliever. I love the game. The strategy. The skill. Being outside with friends. Everything about it. There are so many layers to golf that make it such a compelling game, but the simple act of combining your knowledge of what needs to be done with actually pulling off the shot makes golf the best, in my humble opinion.

I've played some amazing courses that are beautiful, challenging, and distinct. One of the most beautiful—and by far one of the hardest—is the Ocean Course at Kiawah Island. Eleven holes are on the ocean and are exposed to the wind and weather. The Ryder Cup was held there in 1991. Rory McIlroy won the PGA Championship there in 2012. This course constantly ranks in the top five most difficult in the country.

So, it only makes sense that the Ocean Course was on my golf bucket list. It just so happened that in 2012 my family decided to vacation on Kiawah Island (my wife and I honeymooned there, so it means a lot to us). The PGA Championship was scheduled for August that year, and we were there in May. If you know anything about golf courses, you know that those who maintain them make them perfect—and often harder—before major championships are played. It was in the best condition possible. With my wife's incredible grace, I paid way too much money to try my game at one of the best courses in the world.

When you play well-known and expensive golf courses, you often have to book a caddie. Caddies do many things, but the key ones are keeping golfers from playing too slowly and helping them understand the nuances of the course. Especially if they've never played there before.

Without a caddie at the Ocean Course, I very well could still be there playing! For me, using a caddie wasn't so much for the speed of the round. His assistance in reading the greens was helpful, but that was not the greatest benefit either. It was simple: he pointed me in the right direction.

There were so many blind shots that, without having played the course before, I'd probably have ended up hitting to completely wrong fairways or greens. The caddie was an expert. He'd spent so many days playing, walking, and evaluating the course that he understood its uniqueness. Because he'd seen enough shots that were great on one day and terrible on the next, the caddie had clarity for most situations, even among changing conditions. Golf is one part hitting the shot. The other—and maybe more important—factor is knowing where and how far to hit the shot!

Here's my point: evaluated experience gives leaders understanding, which leads to wise decisions. Said another way . . .

*Leaders who evaluate can make decisions right out of the gate!*

You might say you know how to hit good shots. So, let me be your caddie for a while. I want to point you in the right direction for evaluation: Where to look. What to look for. How to do this in a healthy way.

## Safety Takes No Holidays

I'm not going to spend too much time here because I've already covered this at length. If you don't create a safe place for evaluation, you will never get the best from your new team. This is true 100 percent of the time. (Obviously, I made that number up, but I believe it's true, so I'm standing by the statistic!)

I've never seen an organization become a life-giving and successful long-term enterprise if the culture is unsafe for staff to share their thoughts. I have seen plenty of counterfeits, where the leadership team believed the staff felt they were safe to say what they needed to but it wasn't actually true. The lack of emotional intelligence and self-perception from the top down was staggering.

If you are taking over something you didn't start and you have responsibility for any team or product, then you'd better learn how to create a safe evaluation space.

## WE EVALUATE THE IDEA, NOT THE PERSON

I'm not sure I'd ever understood the pain of artists, musicians, and writers more than when I handed the first chapter of my first book to my wife and two other people for the first time. They had in their hands my unique thoughts. My perspective. It was my version of a song written or a picture painted. Whom did I hand the first draft to? Safe friends. Leaders whose evaluation and criticism were geared not toward me personally but toward making the manuscript better than I could make it myself.

---

Fresh eyes and friendship make
a great formula for evaluation.

---

When you can combine fresh eyes and skills with kind and caring relationships in order to look at ideas from different perspectives, you will be one of the healthiest organizations or teams around. It's what chapter 2 was all about—the fruit of the Spirit. You exhibit the fruit of the Spirit in this context, and God will honor your hard work and heavy lifting when it comes to evaluation. Plus, your team and the organization will get better in the process!

The absolute hardest part of evaluation is understanding how to accomplish this well in a large group meeting. There we are evaluating ideas, not people. Let me be very clear about this. There's a time and place for evaluating people, and it must happen. That's not optional. Evaluating team members on a regular basis actually speaks value to them. And doing it with some regularity is best. If you choose to evaluate only once a year, then when you give feedback, it will be more discouraging than helpful because you will be pulling from a relational well that hasn't been filled up. If you evaluate the performance of team members regularly and continue to coach them throughout the year, then the annual evaluation will be more of the same.

Your team needs to know you are for them. You're their advocate day in and day out. Most individuals who want to grow welcome feedback. I've learned that when you step into a new space, though, evaluation just requires your *time* to start with. Building trust is a basic skill you'll need for moving the group to a new place. If you don't model for your new peers or direct reports that you want to know them—their leadership skills, their wiring, even their Enneagram types—they will always stay a safe distance from you. But if you can prove you are for them, you'll fight beside them, and you're in it to see them succeed and grow through evaluation, you will have loyal, productive team members for a long time.

Back to evaluating ideas. One of my favorite books for professionals, which I referenced earlier, is *The War of Art* by Steven Pressfield. He has an amazing way of summing up this concept of evaluation and how to not take it personally:

> A professional schools herself to stand apart from her performance, even as she gives herself to it heart and soul. . . .
>
> The professional loves her work. She is invested in it wholeheartedly. But she does not forget that the work is not her. . . .
>
> The professional self-validates. She is tough-minded. In the face of indifference or adulation, she assesses her stuff coldly and objectively. Where it fell short, she'll improve it. Where it triumphed, she'll make it better still. She'll work harder. She'll be back tomorrow.
>
> The professional gives an ear to criticism, seeking to learn and grow.[1]

I love that line: "She does not forget that the work is not her." How many of us need to hear that? That's a life-giving way to lead. Be yourself. The work isn't you. Hopefully, the work is a positive reflection of you, your skills, and your character. But the job doesn't define you. It's just work.

Good gracious, if we leaders could understand our work like this! It seems to be much harder for leaders in mission or ministry roles where the work aligns with who they are and their calling. Their work is difficult to separate from their identity because it's so deeply rooted in their hearts. Honestly, after years of serving in ministry and being connected to leaders whose identity is inseparable from their work, I can completely understand why this is such a challenge. Let me be transparent: I'm going through this myself right now.

As I'm writing this book, I'm in a season of major life transition. My days of leading Catalyst are over. My identity is no longer as the leader of Catalyst. I'll always be connected to the organization, but it's no longer my title. That's weird. I have learned the power and importance of grieving a change in identity. It doesn't make a difference if you're going to something even better than your former role. It's a loss, a hit on your identity. The new place and role are not the same. Life has changed. If you don't recognize this change, you might regret it later. All this is to say that you and your work can be separated, even though sometimes it doesn't feel that way.

The leader's job is to reiterate this concept daily. We have to explain that when we offer feedback, we are evaluating the idea, project, or event, not the person. If the idea didn't work, we can't be afraid to say that, because the leader needs to be a truth teller.

Over the years I have had many ideas fail miserably. But that didn't keep me from trying again. If I never looked hard at the failure, then I would never get better. I'd never understand why something didn't work. If I always felt like people were personally attacking me, not critiquing the idea, then it would be impossible for me to stick my neck out again with more new ideas.

Have you ever been in a culture where evaluation was survival of the fittest? Some leaders just love to argue and fight and tear down ideas without a posture of grace or the EQ to realize how unproductive that is for a team. They are usually the same leaders who have a hard time not believing that their ideas are the best, and they will circle back to them multiple times. And after their condemning behavior, they wonder why the group isn't excited about their ideas!

That's why it is so important to create an understanding of what evaluation will be like. How it will go down. How to look at the idea and not make it about the person. If you come in with guns blazing and do not handle yourself well, your inherited influence will be short lived.

## Make Decisions on Sunday and Evaluate on Monday

For years I worked in a church with services every Sunday. I was the leader, and there were times on Sunday when I had to make spur-of-the-moment calls, decisions that were best for everyone. In the moment, we didn't have time for a complete evaluation. We had to decide and move on. This wasn't our opportunity to have long conversations and to brainstorm. Decisions had to be made on the go.

It was clear to the church staff that sometimes I would make a decision they might not understand but that we would evaluate it the next day. We would talk through all the options. We would dissect why I made that call and evaluate my decision. I needed to learn and see whether I was making good decisions in the moment.

I tell you this because it's an important concept for someone who walks into an existing tribe or group. Learning the rhythms of the organization and knowing the moments when you have to make decisions and move on will be massive for your new leadership. The problem with many leaders is they never do the second part. You have to close the loop and evaluate. Consistently. Many will make decisions immediately and never follow up with evaluation. That's poor leadership.

## Evaluation Is Not a Nice-to-Have; It's a Must-Have

Every great organization that lasts has learned the art of evaluation. You don't get to be great without it. When you are leading something you didn't start, you need a road map to figure out where you and the group are going. Without evaluation, you'll never know how to hit your tee shot! If you don't know what's currently working, what's failing, and what might be salvaged with proper focus, how will you ever know how to lead?

As I mentioned earlier, the last section of this book includes interviews with great leaders who have stepped into huge roles in organizations they didn't start. Cheryl Bachelder, former CEO of Popeyes, is one. She talked about the importance of giving your new team a road map. Directions. Where are we going?

No one wants to follow a leader who isn't clued in to where the organization needs to go!

Now that we have foundational thoughts on why and how evaluation works, here are some practical questions for evaluating something you didn't start:

> What's currently the best thing going for us?
> What are the obstacles that need to be removed?
> What's worked in the past that no longer works as well now?
> What's worked in the past that we need to go back to?
> How's the team doing with the objectives?
> What's missing that would equip the team to make better decisions?
> What are we afraid of?
> What are some "old couches" that are evident early on?
> What is the market saying about our product?
> Where can we find more information to solve a problem?
> What areas need change but something unspoken is going on with them?
> What are we best at?
> Where is it clear that we are struggling?
> What's our target?
> What does the team think the target is?
> How do we know whether we are winning?
> What are the hills we will die on?

These questions are a starting spot, but you will have to figure out the relevant specifics. There's no cookie-cutter formula for evaluating what you've inherited. I do know one thing: if you lead well in the beginning, the rest of your leadership will be so life giving that you and the team will never be the same!

## QUICK QUESTIONS

1. Which area needs your focus and evaluation first?

2. Which question from the list should get your attention today?

# Section 3

## PATIENCE DICTATES THE SUCCESS OF INHERITANCE: THREE KEYS TO WAITING

WE LIVE IN A WORLD THAT DOESN'T LIKE TO WAIT. I DON'T LIKE TO WAIT. I KNOW you don't. But Jesus never said we should look or act like the world.

Patience is one of the nine fruits of the Spirit. For leaders who are inheriting something they didn't start, it could be the difference between leading well and crashing. Over the next three chapters, I'm going to do my best to give you a framework for focusing on the future while staying patient in the present. In your new organization, some fires will have to be put out immediately, but most of the issues will take time to address and fix.

Music often pierces my heart with truths I need to keep. A couple of years ago when I first heard "Seasons" by Hillsong Worship,[1] I had to stop what I was doing because the song brought tears to my eyes. It might be a great exercise for you to stop reading for a few minutes, pull up your favorite platform for music, and listen to this song. I believe it will put your heart in the right place for these next three chapters.

As you continue into this new section, hopefully you'll start noticing a plan appearing that can be replicated as we move forward. It's going to be a great acronym you can use anytime you step into something you didn't start. Here's the first half of the acronym:

> **E**—Evaluation
> **P**—Patience

Let's hurry up and wait!

# 7

## STAY CONNECTED:
## A RELATIONSHIP WITH JESUS

*Live in me. Make your home in me just as I do in you. In
the same way that a branch can't bear grapes by itself
but only by being joined to the vine, you can't bear fruit
unless you are joined with me.*

—JOHN 15:4, MSG

HAVE YOU EVER FELT LIKE YOU WERE COMPLETELY SEPARATED FROM OTHERS?
Ever had that feeling of being around people but with no connection?
Ever felt like the relationships that are most important and make you
your best self were off, and it was hurting you and your leadership?

Do I have a story for you . . . about me.

The year after I graduated from the University of Georgia, I stuck
around and interned at the Wesley Foundation. Wesley was the campus ministry I was involved in, and it served as an important season of
my life. Deep spiritual growth and the start of lifelong friendships char-
acterized my five years of involvement with the foundation.

It's also where I met my wife, Carrie.

When I was interning, Carrie and I got serious about our relationship and started dating. We dated on and off, but I broke up with her a
couple of times. (That's right: I broke up with her twice and still can't tell
you exactly why . . . other than being an idiot!) Many of our mutual
friends took her side in the *West Side Story* remake—and rightfully so. I
would've, too, if I hadn't been the one responsible for the heartbreak!
It's what friends are supposed to do: support their friend, even if that
means no longer talking to the other party.

As tough as that was, the situation we found ourselves in was quite complicated. When we got back together the first time, I was preparing to lead a mission trip to Alaska. She decided to go on the trip, along with many of our close friends. For the ten weeks leading up to the trip, we all met together as a team, and I led us in prayer and planning. It was shaping up to be an amazing trip!

And then, as mentioned before, I broke up with her again. This was the second time in less than a year.

Now we had a slight problem. I was leading this trip, and everyone in the group had decided I was a jerk (again, rightfully so). *Let the fun begin!* The weekly meetings weren't terrible, but they weren't great either. It was becoming quite obvious that I was about to be on a friend island . . . alone.

The trip went off as planned. Me. Sixteen others. Occasionally, one or two of the students who had an ounce of empathy would check in on me or ride in the van I drove. No kidding. We had two vans, and one was called the party van. That wasn't my van. Here's the weirdest part. I was on a trip with sixteen other people and felt completely on my own. It was like I was watching the trip happen as an observer, not a participant. Similar to watching *Big Brother* but being on it at the same time. I'm not sure I've ever been less connected while being with people. I tell you this story not to shame the others—again, I completely deserved the cold shoulder—but to make the point that, without staying connected to the right relationships, you'll miss the opportunities in front of you.

To this day Carrie and I still get together with some of the friends who were on the trip, and they all laugh about this moment or that. And I sit and smile because I remember only about 5 percent of the stories they tell. I wasn't a part of the others.

Have you ever felt like this with God? I can remember seasons when I was going through hard times or trying to lead well but felt something was off. I would be looking all over for answers, like I'd lost my phone or laptop.

*Listen up!* I'm not sure there's ever been a moment in a book when I wished more that I could take you by the shoulders, look you in the eye, and drive a point deep into your spirit. *Without a constant connection to God, you will not be able to lead at the level you're called to lead!*

Another way to say this:

*Your source will dictate your course.*

For me, it's Jesus.

Whether I'm leading my family at home, spending time developing my friendships, or working my tail off to serve leaders in a church or the marketplace, Jesus has to remain central to my life. When I stay connected to Him, I have the fruit of the Spirit as I lead and I also have direction. I feel connected and not alone.

I feel led. That's a crazy thought: *feeling led by God while I lead for God.*

So, why am I talking about this right now? Aren't we learning about leading things you didn't start? Yep.

There are two reasons I'm bringing this up right now:

1.  I have your attention, and anytime we can be reminded that we need to stay plugged in to our heavenly Father, we should take it.
2.  There is absolutely *zero* chance we will be able to truly lead through a new season in an organization we didn't start and remain patient as long as necessary—in our own strength.

Patience is so difficult. Some of us are more patient than others. However, when it comes to *ourselves* and the things we want to accomplish, it's another story. Is it just me, or are you able—without a lot of work—to muster patience or grace with other people? I get that there are some circumstances that are so extreme that patience was lost a long time ago. But for the most part, I think we are pretty good at patience when it comes to others. When it affects us? *Yuck.* Here's my story:

When I feel like I know what's best, I'm ready to move.

When I see the potential, I'm ready to move.

When it benefits me or others, I'm ready to move.

Usually before God is ready for me to move.

What is the foundational discipline required to be patient in this season of leading something you didn't start? *Connection to God.*

> Inspection without connection could lead
> in the wrong direction.

Your patient inspection and evaluation of the situation must be a critical part of your leadership plan.

Have you ever had a moment when you were thinking about going a certain way or taking a particular action and you felt that little nudge, that small voice leading you somewhere else? If you are not connected to Jesus, you will find yourself missing these God whispers. His directions. His peace leading your spirit about where to go and what to do. What if God has something to say about the direction or the timing that would serve the situation and the team better?

> Waiting while disconnected and alone is horrible.
> Waiting while connected is manageable.

I'm not sure I could ever say waiting is great or satisfying or fun. It's just not. Is the reward we are waiting for amazing? Probably. Is the process of growth worth the wait? Yes. How about the waiting itself? Not usually great. Manageable at best.

Patience is a fruit of the Spirit because if waiting were easy to do, we wouldn't need the Spirit's help. Waiting for God's timing requires complete connection to and trust in the Spirit. Instead of getting ahead of yourself or the team, you stay in step with God.

It's hard enough to wait while connected to the living God. How much more difficult will it be if you do it alone? It goes back to the dance. He takes a step; you take a step. You step before He does, and the dance gets messed up.

## THE BOYS IN THE BOAT

A few years ago, my wife introduced me to the amazing story told in the book *The Boys in the Boat*. It's the unbelievable story of the US rowing team who competed at the 1936 Berlin Olympics. Few stories have had a greater impact on my soul than this incredible tale. Here's why I bring it up now. If any of the boys in the boat would've got disconnected or out of sync, even just the slightest, the team would have lost. Instead, perfect rhythm. Perfect timing. Perfect trust.

Each rower had to trust that the boy in front of him and the boy behind him would stay in sync. Do you have any idea how many hours of rowing it requires to get that connected? Me neither, but after I read this book, my respect for what these young men accomplished went through the roof. The sacrifice of constantly working to tighten the connection. Hours spent practicing one move. Days fine-tuning the length of strokes. The team became a perfect machine.

Not to get too snarky, but how many great leaders do you know who are spending this kind of energy and attention to stay in connection with their heavenly Father?

Too many of us believe we can have a two-minute prayer in the car before we go into a situation and know what God wants from us. I'm not trying to be rude or judgmental. This is my story as much as anyone's. I think I can throw up a quick prayer and get connected in time to lead well and make good decisions. That's like jumping into a spot in the middle of the rowing team. You're not even sure how to hold the paddles—let alone in any sort of shape to row all out, in sync, for two minutes!

Do you get my point?

I can't emphasize this enough! Are there additional practical things we need to touch on about inheriting influence? Yes! But not until we build our foundation on solid ground—with the greatest helper, the Holy Spirit, walking with us and speaking to our hearts.

---

> Without a constant, growing relationship with
> Jesus, we could lack the understanding and
> insight God wants to share with us.

---

You might be asking, "Tyler, how are you so confident about this point?"

I would turn that around and ask you, "How has it gone in your life when you've been disconnected and done everything in your own power?"

If you have walked this faith journey any length of time, I believe you've experienced both sides of this coin. Either you make decisions and lead with God's direction and help that come through prayer, community, and study of the Word, or you try to do this all by yourself and isolate and burn out.

Leadership in times of inheriting influence will require more patience and waiting than you want to endure if you are not connected to God's direction. There will be so many times when you will want to grab the reins and take off at a gallop. Jesus can help you stay calm and patient. If you gallop too soon, you might get thrown off the horse.

At the risk of talking out of both sides of my mouth, no doubt there are certain inherited situations that will require you to grab the reins quickly, to make hard decisions, and to move pieces or people immediately. I promise you that if you are connected to God and trusting Him with these decisions, it'll be much easier to discern how much of each you'll need to do.

## THE PLANE IS ON FIRE!

I remember when a good friend of mine, Joel Thomas, took over a church in Phoenix, Arizona. He knew he was inheriting a mess. Joel and I had worked together for years at North Point Ministries. I was super excited for him when he got the opportunity to go, but I also prayed he would be given wisdom as he stepped into a rough situation. Rough on many fronts based on the leadership that preceded him and the mess that was left.

I will never forget a great conversation we had about a year into his leadership there. I'd known Joel long enough to know how connected he stays to the Lord. He had a deep understanding of why that connection was so important for leading something he didn't start. Here's my recollection of a principle Joel shared after some experience in that season:

> For the first few months of transition and trying to fix the airplane, I threw every value, cultural change, and leadership idea at the problems. I tried everything I had learned

at North Point that was successful. It didn't work. Some things helped, but for the most part, not much was working. Here's what I realized. *The plane was on fire!* I was trying to put out the fire and fix the plane while it was in the air. I quickly realized that wasn't going to work. My job was to *land* the plane, put the fire out, and then rebuild the plane on the ground.

As Joel learned, *we have to be patient.* We have to get all the fires put out. We can keep trying to make adjustments while we're flying at thirty thousand feet, but it's not going to work.

When you take something over, it will require recalibration, and you can't do that if you are moving too fast. Sometimes the fires are current team members. Oftentimes they are financial. Many times the fire is a horrible leadership culture that has almost ruined great things. You have the opportunity to lead a turnaround.

Patience. It will take well-timed leadership.

I love that picture, though—*land the plane and put out the fires.* Don't come in trying to show off all your skills on day one. Listen. Wait. Trust. Connect. Listen some more.

Waiting stinks. But it's worth it.

Now you're connected. That's the first key in waiting.

## QUICK QUESTIONS

1. When was the last time your dependence on God outpaced just using your brain?

2. How has being patient—without trusting God—gone for you?

# 8

## TRUST THE PROCESS: SEEDS DON'T GROW OVERNIGHT

*Gardens are not made*
*By singing:—"Oh, how beautiful!" and sitting in the*
*shade.*

—RUDYARD KIPLING

MY WIFE AND I MIGHT BE THE WORST COUPLE EVER AT WAITING FOR THE RIGHT time to give a gift. There have been very few Christmases when we actually were able to surprise each other with gifts, because we don't wait to give the gifts! A friend used to refer to both of us as a "johnny jumpstart" when it comes to giving gifts. He said we are always jumping too early.

I don't know why we are like this. Maybe it's part of the psychology of preferring to pick out what we want instead of being surprised? Maybe it's just because waiting stinks and we don't want to do it?

The thing about Christmas and gifts in general is that a well-timed surprise gift certainly is worth waiting for because the payoff is so rewarding! Yet we keep settling for less. Not experiencing a perfectly timed gift, because we opened it too early. Or jumping ahead with a decision that needed a little more time. Is this why credit card debt is at ridiculous levels? Instant gratification is taking the place of patience and waiting. We have settled for less and grown accustomed to doing so.

## THE MARSHMALLOW EXPERIMENT

Our culture wants to make things faster and have them more readily available. But this tendency to want things *now* isn't a new phenomenon.

In the 1960s there was a professor at Stanford University named Walter Mischel who wanted to see where this desire comes from and how it can affect us long term. He created an experiment to watch kids ages four and five make a simple decision. Thus, the marshmallow experiment was born.[1]

The basic goal of the experiment was to see whether young children would wait for a better reward. In an empty room, he would set a single marshmallow on a table, then bring a child in by herself. The facilitator would then explain that if the child could wait and not eat the marshmallow until the facilitator returned, she would receive a second marshmallow as a reward. Sounds simple, doesn't it? The kids were not told how long the facilitator would be gone. The results were pretty much what we might expect. The majority of the children couldn't resist and worked that first marshmallow like a bird eating a worm. A few, however, waited and were rewarded with a second marshmallow.

"I'm okay with just one," you might say.

"One is better than nothing," others might say (including me many times).

Instant gratification is very real and plagues our world. If I'm honest, it's been a struggle for me my whole life and has influenced my leadership. Waiting isn't my favorite thing to do. I can always convince myself of the benefits of acting now instead of waiting. It's so frustrating but also so difficult to stop doing this. Rewards still feel like treats even if they are less than what they *could* be because our need for instant gratification prompted us to settle for an inferior version. One marshmallow is better than zero but not as good as two. So, why don't we wait?

One the most insightful findings from the marshmallow test came years later. It wasn't a huge surprise that kids would jump on the first reward in front of them. But when the same children became adults? Yep. The children who were in the original research group were tracked to see how they had fared in life and whether there was a correlation between how they'd responded in the past and how they made decisions as adults. James Clear curated the results:

> The children who were willing to delay gratification and waited to receive the second marshmallow ended up having higher SAT scores, lower levels of substance abuse, lower likelihood of obesity, better responses to stress, better social skills as reported by their parents, and generally better scores in a range of other life measures.[2]

Unbelievable! Are you kidding me? A test given when kids were four or five to determine how willing they were to wait and trust that waiting would be worth it could predict quite accurately how their lives would turn out? *Crazy!*

Think about it, though. Take money, for example. Think of someone you know who's been faithful with what he's been given since he got out on his own. Someone who's always saved first and then bought only what he could afford. I'm always in awe of leaders who are patient and manage finances right. Mainly because I've seen it done wrong and done it wrong plenty of times. I've fallen for an instant reward here and there. Especially if it involved something fun!

As we look at trusting the process and waiting the right amount of time after stepping into leading something we didn't start, an inability to delay gratification might be the biggest obstacle to our leadership. Listen to how James Clear finished this thought:

> The studies . . . make one thing clear: if you want to succeed at something, at some point you will need to find the ability to be disciplined and take action instead of becoming distracted and doing what's easy. Success in nearly every field requires you to ignore doing something easier (delaying gratification) in favor of doing something harder (doing the work and putting in your reps).[3]

# THE PROCESS DEFINES YOU

A few years ago, we had "Make" as a theme for Catalyst. I loved it because the main idea was simple and gave us so many creative opportunities to develop. Here's one way to explain this:

*The destination isn't what defines you. The process defines you. It* makes *you.*

If there's a message that needs to be dropped deep into the hearts and souls of the emerging generation, it's this one!

The process.

The waiting.

The developing.

The pain.

The growth.

The time.

The experience.

We are all in process. In the next chapter, we will talk about how nothing of value happens overnight. Instant just doesn't happen. If it does occur, it isn't sustainable. The *now* is about the process. Trusting it. Believing that God has your best interests in mind as He allows you to go through the fire. "We know that for those who love God all things work together for good, for those who are called according to his purpose."[4]

After being in leadership for more than twenty years, I am certain of one thing: the process is what defines us.

---

Most destinations are temporary stops
on the lifetime journey of growth.

---

It's no different during a season of transition in which you are owning someone else's influence. How you handle the process of waiting will either make you that much better as a leader or take you out. One marshmallow or two?

I have to confess: even as I'm writing this, I'm convicted of all the times I've chosen the quick route. The seed planted didn't have time to grow into a mature plant. I pulled the fruit off before it was ready. I have a feeling I'm not the only one.

I cannot stress this enough in this discussion of inherited leadership. It's a dance between pushing and patience. Wanting and waiting. Telling leaders what to do and trusting them to do it. As I mentioned, the song "Seasons" by Hillsong Worship is one of my favorite songs ever. Especially for this conversation. I know you've already listened to the song once, but I want to highlight a couple of the lines as we think about the importance of waiting.

Seasons sometimes seem like they are lasting forever, but then they change. I promise you that as you lead something you didn't start, some seasons will seem like a cold winter that never ends. Hold on.

> Though the winter is long, even richer
> The harvest it brings.[5]

God takes His time. Great things take time. Leading takes time. The seed doesn't grow overnight, but when it's ready . . .

## SUPERBLOOM

If we understand trees and most plants, we know that observable growth doesn't happen overnight. Oftentimes seeds will be in the ground for years before any growth shows above the surface. But if a seed lies dormant in the right soil and then the conditions are right, the growth will be something beautiful.

When thousands of seeds germinate after quietly waiting for the conditions to be right, watch out.

In 2016, perfect conditions including heavy rain in Death Valley National Park brought one of the most desolate landscapes to life.[6] Consider this:

> A superbloom is a rare desert botanical phenomenon in which an unusually high proportion of wildflowers whose seeds have lain dormant in desert soil germinate and

blossom at roughly the same time. The phenomenon is associated with an unusually wet rainy season.[7]

Sometimes all that is needed is a rainy season. Have you ever watched a leader who's been dormant for a while open up and step into leadership like a completely new person? I've seen leaders simply need better conditions, and the next thing you know . . . superbloom!

Right now I'm working with a church where the team has been dormant, buried under the soil, for a long season. The conditions haven't been ideal. But with every day we are together, I'm watching a superbloom burst forth because the environment now allows growth. In other words, with proper timing, care, and watering, these leaders are transitioning into the new season of leadership with amazing colors! They are coming to life. They feel seen and valued. And they are showing off!

These leaders now have a voice and a chance to lead and make decisions instead of functioning under a dictatorship that put them back on their heels. The conditions they were working in didn't allow for great leadership opportunities. They were accountable and responsible for many things but given no authority to make decisions.

## PATIENCE DOES NOT EQUAL IDLENESS

There is a massive difference between idleness and patience. Many leaders miss this important piece of the puzzle. Often when we are waiting, we will find ourselves idle. This doesn't mean we can't be doing something! It is just as important to keep planting new seeds as it is to wait for the growth from the first seeds.

I love this quote from the novelist Franz Kafka: "There are two cardinal sins from which all the others spring: impatience and laziness."[8]

We have to keep working and fertilizing even while we are waiting. It's not time to sit on the bench and watch until something grows. We have to work and plant more seeds for the years to come.

Without acting like I know everything about farming, because clearly I do not, I do know how much preparation and work are required to grow even the simplest of crops:

You have to know what and where to plant
  (**E**valuation).
You have to learn the timing for maximizing
  growth (**P**atience).
You have to know how to harvest
  (**I**mplementation).
You have to care for the seeds while they are
  growing (**C**are).

Look. Don't direct message me telling me there's way more to farm-ing than that . . . I know! This is a simple overview, and we will be served well by keeping it simple when we think about stepping in, when we continue to work while waiting for the seeds to grow.

A friend once said that we must work like it depends on us and sleep like it depends on God. That's it. As you lead something you didn't start, you have to trust that when you are faithful to work hard while waiting to see growth, God will honor that. I just don't believe that God honors laziness. He doesn't endorse idleness or laziness in leaders.

## PARABLE OF THE TALENTS

In Matthew 25, there's a famous story about an owner and the team members he asked to invest his money. I love that, instead of money, some Bible versions call the investment "talents," which was a form of money then but means skills and gifting to us today. Anyway, let me give you a quick refresher of what happened.

The owner was leaving for a long trip and had three servants to look after some things for him. To the first he gave five talents. (Note that a talent was significant money. Sometimes a year's wages for a day la-borer would equal one talent. So this isn't like five bucks.) Then he gave another servant two talents, and the last servant he gave one talent.

Now, I have no idea how the owner decided how much to give each of his employees, but it seems like he had discernment about which servant to give which amount to. He knew them. He understood who had earned the right to more weight. More responsibility. More capital.

When the owner returned from his trip, the three servants met with him to report what they'd done with the investment. The first came with the talents doubled from five to ten. The owner was pleased and filled with gratitude. The second servant also returned double the original amount. He, too, had worked diligently and shrewdly to make his talents grow. The last servant, however, was a different story. Listen to how the Bible describes this extremely uncomfortable conversation:

> He also who had received the one talent came forward, saying, "Master, I knew you to be a hard man, reaping where you did not sow, and gathering where you scattered no seed, so I was afraid, and I went and hid your talent in the ground. Here, you have what is yours." But his master answered him, "You wicked and slothful servant! You knew that I reap where I have not sown and gather where I scattered no seed? Then you ought to have invested my money with the bankers, and at my coming I should have received what was my own with interest."[9]

What might have been this man's thoughts? *I was afraid, so I went and hid your money. I did nothing while I waited. I wasted the opportunity to use the one talent that was given to me. Instead I sat under the tree talking about the garden but didn't work on it.*

Fellow leader who is taking over something you didn't start, *this is it.* You are being handed someone's talent. What are you going to do with it? Are you going to sit and watch it out of fear? Or are you going to work and trust that God will be with you?

**E**valuation
**P**atience
**I**mplementation
**C**are

Take your time, but don't sit still. Look around and learn, but don't be lazy. There's too much at stake. Your faithfulness will be rewarded. It just might not be overnight.

## QUICK QUESTIONS

**1.** Where have you tried to jump ahead of the process?

**2.** What needs more time to take root?

# 9

## INSTANT ISN'T SUSTAINABLE: IF GOD'S NOT DONE WORKING, I'M NOT DONE WAITING

*I was an overnight success all right, but thirty years is a long, long night.*

—RAY KROC

YUM. I CAN TASTE THOSE MORSELS OF GOODNESS NOW. THIS MAGNIFICENT food will never be forgotten.

Instant mashed potatoes.

That's right. Delicious. Well . . . something.

I remember this being a common side dish on my family's dinner table. I actually liked them. With a ton of butter and salt. But seriously—take a look at the ingredient list for this nutritious nectar: corn syrup solids, partially hydrogenated soybean oil, sodium caseinate, dipotassium phosphate, sodium silicoaluminate, artificial color, monoglycerides and triglycerides, soy lecithin, and artificial flavor.

I know what sodium is. And the word *artificial*. The rest of the words tell me there isn't a whole lot in there to write home about. Remember our discussion in the previous chapter about good things taking time? These delicious "potatoes" take about a minute.

---

Quick and quality aren't usually
cohorts in our lives.

---

I'm not throwing shade on all things quick. Fast cars are cool (though they take a long time to build). Fast food can be good (Chick-fil-A's process to provide great fast food is excellent). Amazon can get toilet paper to my house in literally an hour (that's another conversation).

You get my point.

A few months ago, I got a Big Green Egg grill, and it's awesome. If you're unfamiliar with this cooker, the Big Green Egg is a grill-smoker-griddle all in one. It's a porcelain wonder of the world. For years, I used a simple gas grill. Please know that I'm not about to dog on the gas grill. However, *this Egg*! Now, as I've already confessed, I do like some things quick. This modern marvel, however, forces me to wait.

A few weeks ago, I smoked my first Boston butt for pulled pork. Barbecue, baby! I had to get up at 5:00 a.m. so I could prepare the Egg to smoke this joker all day. Ten hours. Ten!

No shortcuts allowed. Well, I take that back. You can cook it for a few hours on really high heat and end up with pork jerky that's terrible, or you can do it right. Ten hours on low heat. Time. There's nothing instant about a great pulled-pork meal. You've got to plan, get the meat, season it, let it sit, get the charcoal to the right temperature, have the best tools for holding it, and then start cooking.

During the cooking, you have to regularly check the temperature of both the Egg and the pork. Occasionally adding flavor or moisture is necessary. Even when this bad boy is done, you aren't. You have to pull the meat apart with claws. Finally, after almost twelve hours, it's go time.

You might be wondering right now, *Why in the world is he talking about this?* (And did you get just a little hungry for some barbecue? I did!)

My point: There really isn't anything that is instant that makes the world better. There really aren't overnight successes. Even when you hear of leaders stepping in and turning around companies or churches, it takes time.

*But,* you might think, *I've been waiting a long time already.*

Can you remember times when you thought you were going to have an answer to a problem within days but it turned into waiting for weeks, months, or even years? Most of the time we believe that we know better and can see better than those around us. Sometimes even better than God.

In the past few years, the number of times that I've ended up having to wait significantly longer than I planned or preferred have been too many to count. Each time—and I do mean each time—I thought I knew better. I thought it was going to be a quick fix. I wanted to move on. Nope.

Maybe for you it was waiting longer than expected in one of the following areas:

> Finances
> Friends
> Marriage
> Work
> Grief
> Team development
> Having kids

Any of these areas can make having patience crazy difficult. Here's another section from the song "Seasons":

> If You're not done working,
> God, I'm not done waiting.[1]

I'm not sure I've ever heard lyrics that drove truth so deep into my spirit in this area—or any other, for that matter.

Let's make sure we get it:

> If You're not done working,
> God, I'm not done waiting.

Are we cool?

All right, my job here is done. Pack it up. Let's roll out!

Nah. I know it doesn't work that easily, but it's still true. What if—and I know this a big what-if—in the process of waiting, God has something in store for you?

*Are you serious?*

Yes, I'm dead serious. I know how nasty the wait can be. I know how many times I begged God to answer the question, solve the problem, or fix the situation. I know how many nights I lay awake, telling God what He should do. In the past few years, I've struggled with insecurity in leadership (a new struggle for me), the challenge of managing company owners like I've never faced before, and trying to lead a national platform into a new season and in a new direction with daily obstacles to overcome.

---

Most of us want relief from a hard season,
when what we need is revelation.

---

I raise my hand as guilty on this. Honestly, my desire for the end of waiting usually has to do with a desire for pain to subside. For it to go away. When you take over a mess, there's pain. So many times I've wished I could just wave my hand like a Jedi and make the pain go away for the people I'm leading. But I can't.

Have you ever had seasons like that—when you go through trials you never thought you'd face? In this most recent season, I've had nights of anxiety and fear like never before, when I've lain in the fetal position, wondering whether I was going to make it to the next day. I've been insecure like at no other time in my life and leadership. I can remember days when I thought, *If this door gets closed, I'm done.*

Have you ever had days like that? Years like that?

When I stopped trying to open doors myself and quit viewing God through my current circumstances, I started to see that maybe, just maybe, He was still on the move. I quickly learned that many times a no or closed door is actually an upgraded yes! I can remember four times in about a two-month window when I thought I was done if God didn't open the door in front of me. Hindsight is twenty-twenty, right? Looking back, I now see that if God had opened any of those four doors, I would have been settling for something less than His best.

> The nos in our lives are God's plans to
> get us to the upgraded yeses!

This isn't just a personal devotional message in the middle of a leadership book. It's a truth that has to be understood to lead well in times of transition. Many times you will think you are having to wait too long for God to solve the problem or answer the question. Sometimes you will be so frustrated that the team isn't responding as quickly as you'd hoped or you aren't gaining the influence you expected as quickly as planned.

As you lead through transition, succession, or even taking over a struggling ministry or business, there will likely be many closed doors. There will be doors shut in your face—some quietly, some slammed. It's worth it. Wait. The dawn is coming. The new day will arrive. If it's not the right time yet, it's not the best plan yet.

Just like the completely unnatural ingredients in instant mashed potatoes, if you manufacture outcomes or try to get ahead of God's timing, you will see unnatural, instant, and unsatisfying solutions. They don't last. They don't help you play the long game. They provide only short-term relief.

We have to settle deep in our hearts that short-term, instant solutions will fizzle and often put us in worse situations down the road. Settling for second best isn't any kind of best. Yes, one marshmallow is more than zero, but it's not as good as two. The team you inherited is worth your patience.

## CONCENTRATE WHILE STAYING CALM

Let's get super practical! Here are four areas that will require patience and focused leadership as you move into existing spaces.

### 1. People

Surprised this is the first area that will require patience? As a matter of fact, this area will be the paper that all the other areas are written on.

Without understanding this, you won't be able to move the needle on the other three. Actually, without understanding this, your leadership is always going to be an uphill battle.

If you're a parent, you'll understand this dynamic. Patience isn't one option of many with kids. It's the only option. If you can't find the time to wait until they pick up on what you're teaching them, you'll never give them adequate space to grow into whom you want them to become. I can't tell you how many times I've tried to push my kids to mature faster, move faster, learn faster, or even go to bed faster. (Good luck with that one!) No matter how hard I push, I cannot make them do what I want them to do. Even when I know it's better for them!

But when they finally get it . . .

When they finally show progress . . .

When they step into their uniqueness and the lights start going on . . .

That's when you know it's been worth it. All those hard conversations. All the late nights and tears.

It's the same with the teammates you lead in a new season. The people you inherited. You have to remember—*the team members you inherited have probably been led to lead the way they do.*

If you want to blame them from the get-go, go ahead and lose what little influence you have. I'm serious about this. If you aren't patient enough to coach these team members to do things differently, you don't have any business stepping into something you didn't start.

I've heard horror stories of the new-sheriff-in-town mentality when a leader is taking over. Let's not do that. Treat people like you want to be treated. The foundation of any platform, business, church, or team is people. You have to be patient and lead them with respect.

Let me repeat: the next three items on this list don't matter if you can't build trust with the people who are going to make things happen!

## 2. Passion

You're excited about what's next. You have plans. You can see the future! You just aren't there yet.

Ever had those feelings in a meeting with the team?

What feels to the team like a death of passion will absolutely be an obstacle you will face when leading something you didn't start. Founders of organizations can struggle with this their entire career but especially when they are considering transition or succession.

Imagine starting something that is central to your calling and heart and then leading it for a long time. It's the center of your passion and purpose. You live and breathe it every day. And then it's time to hand it off. That honestly might be the hardest thing a leader ever has to do.

I say this to provide a picture of why passion is such a delicate matter. I know it's easy to clearly see what needs to happen when you're looking in from the outside. Obviously, it's time for some changes to the way things have been done. But for the founder, it's been her life. Does your passion match hers? Does your vision match hers?

Probably not. This is one of the most difficult challenges the church will face in the next couple of decades. There are so many wonderful ministries and churches that were started by amazing leaders in the past thirty years. Who's going to step in? Who can match the leaders' passion and skills, and is that even what's needed for the next thirty years? I know pastors who are scared to death of what might happen to the organization they've spent decades building, because they don't know whom they can hand it to.

This is why the DNA of succession should be part of every leader's makeup. We have to always be handing off opportunities for others to grow. Opportunities to lead. Some emerging leaders might not have matching passion yet because they haven't been handed a chance to feel it! Passion doesn't just happen. It requires a spark. A light. A moment. If you never give your team members chances to experience those moments, then good luck finding someone to match the passion required for succession.

## 3. Plans

Another area that might require waiting and patience is the plans you have. Each of us will come with new ideas and plans to move the team forward. If you don't, then you're not prepared. However, it will require a great amount of discernment and discipline to know when to implement them. Some teams are chomping at the bit to get rolling with new ideas. Others would drown in new plans at the start. It all depends on how the group was led before you got there and how much cleanup is required before moving to the next plan.

In the last section of the book, I include my interview with Buzz Williams (first mentioned in chapter 4). He and his staff went to Texas A&M with very clear plans, but he quickly realized that they were going to have to hit pause on those plans because there was other work to do first. Other fires to put out.

If you try to implement certain plans at the wrong time, even if they are the right plans, it's going to be tough. It might even crush your team forever. You could lose the very team you're trying to win.

## 4. Profit

Last but not least. Last only because you have to embrace the first three—people, passion, plans—with proper perspective or your profit will suffer. But if you embrace them in the right way and in the right timing? Watch out! Up and to the right.

Look. I'm not an idiot. I'm fully aware that you may be working in the profit sector. Nothing wrong with that. Your organization is for profit. Make money. Make even more money. Obviously, if you inherit a team or the leadership of a for-profit business, making profit will be a priority. I'm not ignoring that. What I'm saying is that your focus needs to be on turning the team around. If I were a betting man, I would wager that the previous leader of your new team also focused on money. Everyone has to make it a priority. Clearly. The point is simple. But hear me out.

> When you inherit something you didn't start,
> profits turn around when teams turn around.

I'm not sure I've ever heard a story of profits turning in the right direction if a new leader took over something he didn't start and ignored the realities the team was facing. Maybe it has happened once or twice in history, but I'm not interested in that approach. Here we are talking about stepping in with life-giving leadership. We want to love and care for people while turning a profit. Profit requires great people. Fight hard to be patient with profit while building the people who will help get you there.

## FINAL WORD

We just talked for a long time about patience and waiting. I want to address the question that may be burning in your mind now: *How can I be patient when a staff member isn't competent or we have information that requires us to make a move now?*

I always go back to two thoughts. Andy Stanley's message on trust versus suspicion is my starting point. When there's a gap in information ("You are late but we don't know why" or "You missed deadlines but it's unclear what happened"), are we going to choose trust or are we going to choose suspicion? Here's how that coincides with this subject: If we discover there are issues with poor leadership and decision-making, then we have no choice but to act. We have to lead. Sometimes it's clear that a person needs to move on. There are individuals who shouldn't be there, and no amount of patience will solve the problem because they are wrong for the team.

The other thought has to do with moving the team forward. If you step into something you didn't start and there is a toxic player, it will quickly become very clear that something has to change—and soon. My advice is to pray for the fruit of the Spirit to be displayed as you make changes. It could be the best influence-building opportunity for you early in your new space. When a team sees that you are going to build a culture that doesn't allow toxic behavior, they will see that you're a leader worth following.

Now that we've been patient, it's time to build.

## QUICK QUESTIONS

**1.** In which of the four areas were you going for the instant fix?

**2.** How can you work to repair that area?

# Section 4

---

## IMPLEMENTATION: HOW TO SHIFT YOUR CULTURE, CAST VISION, AND MODEL WHAT SUCCESS LOOKS LIKE

MY KIDS WOULD PROBABLY SAY THAT I'M AN OVEREXPLAINER. SOMETIMES I think they are right. There's something about teaching my children a new skill or job that causes me to overexplain. I can see it on their faces when they are done with explanation and ready to try for themselves.

As bad as I am at keeping explanations short, I'm worse at receiving instruction. I'm ready to try something out after about 25 percent of the teaching. There's a reason I believe patience is a fruit of the Spirit and not a natural human characteristic. It's not easy.

So, enough of the explaining already. It's time. Time to move beyond principles to practice. Time to get our hands dirty. Time to quit talking and act.

This section will give you nuts-and-bolts explanations that should help you move the needle in the existing organization.

No more flight simulator for you. It's time to fly.

# 10

## THE CULTURE GAME

*A culture is strong when people work with each other,*
*for each other. A culture is weak when people work*
*against each other, for themselves.*

—SIMON SINEK

ROLLER SKATING. IT'S MY FAVORITE. I TOLD THIS TO A YOUNGER FRIEND RE-cently, and he had no words. He'd never been to a roller rink. He said, "You mean in-line skates?"

Nope. Quads, baby. Four wheels. Neon laces. Speed skates. Incredible music. Advance bounce skating. Couples' skating. "The Hokey Pokey." You name it . . . I loved it about skating. Well, I still love it.

So, when I was turning forty and Carrie asked me what kind of party I wanted?

No-brainer. A skating party.

We rented the entire place and invited some of my favorite people in the world. Now, it's vital to have a proper combination of peak skating conditions. Just like snow skiing needs the right mix of mountains, friends, snow, and sun, skating needs perfect conditions for a perfect skate. You have to create the mood.

Perfect conditions include . . .

Skates that fit properly
Delicately waxed hardwood floors
Ms. Pac-Man making noise on the sidelines
The smell of cheese for nachos

Relay races
Tube socks
Last but not least, the greatest beats the world
   has ever heard

If you don't have a great playlist of skating-specific music, forget about it. That would be like swimming without water, skiing without snow, and playing tennis without rackets. In other words, it's not going to happen.

For my fortieth, I wasn't going to let this music playlist of beauty be curated by a seventeen-year-old who listened only to Taylor Swift and One Direction. I worked night and day on my skating playlist. For two months.

At the office, I'd try out a few of the songs to see whether they got people singing along or bouncing their shoulders. By the way, when curating the perfect skating playlist, you will need to have a certain ear for and understanding of what you're listening for. (I know you are probably just getting ready to curate a skating playlist and that's why you're reading this leadership book. I'm here for you. I like to help in more ways than one.)

What you're listening for is the right beat. A beat that would make some advance bounce skaters look like Bow Wow in *Roll Bounce*! (If you haven't seen the movie . . . you haven't seen the movie.)

For your knowledge, here is a list of the top five skating songs of all time, in my humble opinion:

1. "Word Up"—Cameo
2. "Lookout Weekend"—Debbie Deb
3. "Let the Music Play"—Shannon
4. "Bust a Move"—Young MC
5. "You Give Love a Bad Name"—Bon Jovi

Now that I've enlightened you about the most critical elements of a great skating experience, let me tell you why this is in this leadership book.

If we decided to have a great skating party without proper work and setup and if we didn't have conditions and space that would allow for an extraordinary experience, the time would be wasted.

Picture this: A junky hardwood floor. No AC. Wheels on the skates that keep catching like the sticky ones on grocery carts. Little to no food—definitely no nacho cheese. No arcade games glowing like beacons in the night. And the very, very worst: quiet. Deadly silence. Just the sound of nasty skates scraping against an unkept floor. No music. No beat. No culture.

---

Without creating the best space possible *for* your team, you will never get the best *from* your team.

---

There are a million—okay, a bunch—of books on culture and how it creates competitive advantage. It's been proven time and time again that when you create an environment for flourishing, your people might actually flourish. I know that sounds simple, but it's true. And simple. You cannot expect teams to flourish without building space for them to take off. Just as you can't expect a good skating party without the essentials.

So, here are the essentials, in my mind, for changing the culture you inherited to a culture that allows your people to thrive. These are the basics. I would say these are nonnegotiable items for a team or an organization that I'm leading. I pray they will become foundational for you as well.

One last thought before we talk about each pillar of culture. Some of these can't wait. When you step into something you didn't start, oftentimes you will be forced to make some quick changes so that the environment shifts and expectations get reset. As we go through my list, I'll point out which pillars need to be set first.

## BUILD YOUR CULTURE FOUNDATION ON THESE PILLARS

As I mentioned earlier, my wife and I spent our honeymoon on Kiawah Island, which is just south of Charleston, South Carolina (same location as the Ocean Course). Come to think of it, most of our special moments as a couple have revolved around the beach. Carrie has always loved architecture, and that part of the country has some unreal homes. The interesting difference I've noticed in the architecture as we near the beach is that many of the homes are built on pillars. Unlike inland homes built on a basement or a crawl space foundation, the beach homes are built up eight to ten feet to be ready for hurricanes or tidal issues.

Imagine trying to build a strong beach house if one of the pillars were missing. You are building and know it's missing, but you keep going and try to make it work. It won't.

That's how important each pillar is on my list of how to construct a solid foundation for the new culture you want to establish.

Don't forget. There will be a dance. When you are handed the keys to the culture that already exists, you will have to evaluate which essential pillars already exist but need some tweaking and which pillars are nowhere to be found.

Enough setup! Let's build this house!

## Healthy

When you clear the land and get ready to build a foundation, you have to have a starting spot. Builders decide which corner of the foundation to start with and then build off that. In old buildings, it was sometimes called the cornerstone—the first rock laid to make sure the rest of the foundation was built correctly.

I believe the foundation of a great work culture starts with the pillar of health. *Healthy* can describe a multitude of characteristics, but the questions below focus on several key areas. Of all the pillars, this might be the easiest to figure out almost immediately. (There will be parts of the organization that will remain hidden for a while because all the team members are putting their best foot forward for the new leader. Stand by.)

> The leader's job, when she is handed the keys
> to the existing team or organization, is to
> ruthlessly excavate the unhealthy layers
> of past cultural norms that are keeping the
> group from flourishing.

If you have stepped more than once into something you didn't start, you know what I'm talking about. Within minutes you can hear comments, see body language, and feel fear and even cynicism that indicate a struggle ahead. The real behind-the-scenes culture can be hidden for only so long.

As we learned earlier, if the plane is on fire, land it and put the fire out. When you inherit something you didn't start, carry a fire extinguisher. You will have some fires to put out.

If you have a team member who is toxic and killing the culture, let him go.

If you have terrible processes that no one believes help the business, change them.

Again, you have fresh eyes for only so long, so dig deeply and quickly. Ask around about the culture and see what the team sees. This will help you learn what truly needs to be fixed and what the team no longer sees as a problem. Here are four questions to help you understand the state of the culture.

### Q1: IS THE CURRENT CULTURE A CULTURE OF TRUST OR SUSPICION?

The entire thesis of Patrick Lencioni's book *The Five Dysfunctions of a Team* is that teams must be built on the foundation of trust.[1] If you determine early on that the old culture was built on anything but trust, start there. This will be your cornerstone for rebuilding the organization. It doesn't matter whether you have a super small team or a huge group. You have to show that, without team members trusting one another, goals will never be achieved. So many leaders focus immediately on the numbers. On the metrics. I believe you will never move the needle on metrics, profit, and numeric goals without a healthy, high-functioning team.

### Q2: HOW'S THE GOSSIP?

*Really, Tyler? Gossip? This isn't like a small group of friends hanging out. Why does gossip matter?*

It matters because it's a sign of something deeper. Something further down in the environment. Probably a result of what the past leadership allowed to happen or the way the leaders led. Gossip says that we don't trust the decisions being made or the leadership that's making them.

Best way to curb it? Make a clear expectation for everyone on the staff: "If you're going to be on this team moving forward, you don't talk about anyone without having talked to her first. If you come to me as your leader and haven't first talked directly to the person in question, we won't talk until you do."

A healthy culture sees every person as someone with value. Someone who matters. Your team members deserve to be treated kindly and with respect.

### Q3: Is There a Clear Understanding of Lines We Won't Cross in Doing Business or Ministry?

The fate of this team or business you just inherited will depend on ethical decision-making. Getting a clear picture of what has happened before through research and asking great questions will show you what you need to know.

This is so important if you take over something that is coming off a moral failure, financial implosion from unethical choices with money, or some other ethical downfall. You have no choice but to make sure the team is above reproach in how they are operating and making decisions.

Hopefully by now, you're seeing why the health pillar has to be at the corner. You won't get the honest answers you need until the leaders feel safe and feel they can trust you.

### Q4: Are Staffers Making Decisions Only to Please the Boss?

Remember the WWJD—What Would Jesus Do?—bracelets from the nineties? You may be stepping into a place where everyone is wearing a bracelet like that but with the name of the boss instead of Jesus. Insecure leaders create cultures that force their teams into just pleasing the boss. This kind of leadership keeps team members from bringing their best to the table. It keeps a trust culture from being built, up and down the organizational chart.

If you ask questions about why certain things are done certain ways and the only answer is "Because the boss likes it that way," dig deeper. Ask your new team what they would do. Evaluate whether it's the best way to do it.

One of the quickest ways to gain influence in your new space is to empower the existing team to make wise decisions. See what they see, and coach them to see what you see. Don't just come in and dictate everything. Get their input.

If they've been wearing WWBD bracelets for years, watch how quickly they come out of their shells and start leading creatively!

It's our job as leaders to create and change culture. A healthy culture is foundational for building a house that endures.

## Heard

Now that we understand that we are going to fight for health and that it will dictate the way we build the foundation of our culture, we must put in place the second pillar.

---

You will never change culture if
your team isn't heard.

---

Okay. I'm going to give you one of my personal leadership secrets. Really, I'm serious. This is leadership gold and might be one of the simplest pillars to create. Let your team be heard. How? Glad you asked!

### No Rhetorical Meetings

Have you ever been to a meeting where it was obvious from the start that the leader wanted to "collaborate" but had already decided what was going to happen? Terrible leadership. It's inauthentic and dumb. The leader isn't getting the best out of his team, and the team will never feel heard if the leader continues to have pointless meetings.

Rhetorical meetings are like asking your wife where she'd like to eat and then going to a place that you had already picked. You might be able to do that once or twice but not much longer. She won't even indulge your question when she becomes wise to your self-centered decision-making.

It's no different with your work relationships. People are smart and discerning. They also understand when they aren't being heard. It stinks. Don't waste their time.

## CELEBRATION

Celebration has to be mixed into the concrete that makes the "heard" pillar. It has to be in the DNA of your culture. It must be strategic and not haphazard. You can't just be walking to an all-staff meeting and remember, *Oh yeah, I need to celebrate someone today!*

Maybe celebrating is not natural for you. I understand that you feel like your team is celebrated by getting a paycheck. And, yes, we are all grateful for the paycheck, but people also want to be part of something that matters. We want to be seen and celebrated. We want to feel like we matter. Sometimes we want to hear from our leader that we are doing things right.

---

What gets celebrated paints the picture
of what success looks like.

---

Don't celebrate just the huge product launches or fourth-quarter numbers. Celebrate when a team member treats a teammate with respect. Celebrate that an employee solved an issue because she took initiative. Stories will build healthy culture quicker than anything. I love asking team members in an all-staff meeting to brag on someone else and tell us the story of what they saw a colleague do that aligns with our culture.

I've talked in messages and workshops about how God gave me a unique idea early in my career that has been a huge celebration tool. You might read this and think I'm crazy . . . and I am a little. However, this works! It's more than just celebration. It's reminding team members that they are important to me. Ready?

Occasionally, I'll send thank-you notes and small gifts to the spouses of my employees. Yep, I write thank-you notes to people who don't even work in the office. But, in an important sense, they do work with us and are part of the team. They need to be seen and know that they matter too. It's one of the greatest gifts I've given to the families of my team.

When we would have busy seasons at Catalyst, I would thank the spouses for understanding and holding down the fort at home. The truth is that without their sacrifices *here,* we could not have served thousands of leaders *out there.* In essence, the spouses were serving the same number of leaders as we were.

Most parents would say, "If you want to do something nice for me, do something nice for my kids." Same sentiment with these thank-you notes. Staffers feel heard and seen when their family feels the same.

## Hungry

As soon as I hear that word, I think of Chick-fil-A. *Don't judge me!* Next, I start thinking about what defines hungry teams and why this matters for recreating culture. If you don't have team members whose hunger to grow and get better matches yours, that might be a deal breaker. You can tell pretty quickly who's hungry to push the team and themselves forward. It's equally easy to see who doesn't have a hunger to push. A hunger to grow.

> If your people aren't hungry, then they probably aren't driven by something deeper. We have to awaken that something deeper to get the best out of each person.

I think it's only appropriate to give my friend Brad Lomenick a little love. Especially since he's the guy who handed me the keys to Catalyst and I've learned a ton of great leadership from him. When writing a book on leading things you didn't start, you may be inclined to leave the leader you took over for nameless. Not the case here. Brad has been a longtime friend. He and I have some similar qualities (humor, good looks) but some different leadership gifts as well. We lead some spaces very differently and many the same. I'm grateful for Brad and his belief and investment in me.

Here's why I bring this up right now. Brad has a book called *H3 Leadership: Be Humble, Stay Hungry, Always Hustle.* It's an awesome leadership conversation around some of the key character traits of great leaders. If you want to read more about staying hungry, do yourself a favor and read that!

For our conversation, here are two main ideas about being hungry.

## PASSION

Passion drives us. If you aren't passionate, you aren't hungry.

---

Passion is the oil that keeps the team's
engine running strong.

---

What if your inherited culture is passionless? The team is so beaten down that they've lost the fire in their bones that used to drive them to achieve? Without something that energizes the group, you'll have a hard time moving this team to greatness. You need passion. Where has the passion gone for these team members? What's missing? Your job is to help them find it again. Some of them haven't been passionate for so long that they might not know what it is anymore. Help them figure it out. Without passion, the next piece will be pointless.

## PURPOSE

If passion is the oil, then purpose is the engine. It's the mechanism that creates movement and momentum for your team.

---

People without purpose
are not dynamic difference makers;
they are just hired workers.

---

The world is full of workers who just punch the clock, do the basics required to get paid, punch out, and go home. That's not going to cut it. I honor team members who are faithful to their work and who accomplish the task at hand. The problem is that without purpose or meaning behind their work, it's just work. It's not a mission. It's not something that moves them to be the best and to make those around them the best.

Your mission is to help your team see the bigger purpose. The *why* behind the *what*.

## Hardworking

This fourth pillar should also be a standard when it comes to your team. Yes, we are creating workplaces that are filled with passionate people of purpose, not just workers. However, there is work to do. We will never reach our goals without hard work!

---

> Hard work should be the standard
> operating procedure. Laziness is a virus
> that kills productivity.

---

I feel like I'm giving you all my leadership secrets, but I guess that's the point! Anyway, one additional free truth for you is that there's a reason we are building a healthy culture. When staff members are in a healthy place and feel like they can be their best, they work hard. It's true. Oftentimes if there's a discrepancy between their work ethic now and what it should be, it's the fruit of a poor leadership culture. The environment stinks. Who gets inspired to work hard if the space they're in is toxic?

It's impossible for your employees to be dedicated and hardworking when they feel their work doesn't matter. Motivation will always be a driving force for productivity.

All this to say, an expectation has to be set early on in your tenure that working hard is not simply an option. It's a standard. It's a key part of your culture of greatness.

One quick side note: There is a culture on the opposite end of the spectrum that leads to workaholics and burnout. Rhythm matters for a healthy leadership culture. Leaders who understand when to push their team to work more, as well as when to send them home, will gain influence for years to come. If you come into a culture that has been crushed by working *too* much, then finding that right balance of work and play, focus and rest will be very important in your first few months.

## Honoring

I think Simon Sinek's quote at the beginning of this chapter sets this pillar up better than I can. "A culture is strong when people work with each other, for each other. A culture is weak when people work against each other, for themselves."

I won't spend a ton of time on this because I've already emphasized at length the importance of honoring the past. However, creating a culture of honor builds a place of respect and safety. It's where a team believes in one another and communicates that belief. There are great people in amazing organizations that believe in their teammates but never take the time to tell them! You have to. Put others first. Honor their work. Care about what they care about. Respect their opinions and voices.

In chapter 16, Pastor Jimmy Rollins talks more about this subject in a super practical and helpful way based on what he learned taking over a church from his parents.

We are in this together.

It's often said that time is one resource we never get more of. I know that to be true. We spend a high percentage of our time at work, with the people we work alongside and in the culture of our workplace. I want to be around people whom I like and who share my work culture values. My theory is simple on this point: if I honor people, they will honor me in return.

## Hopeful

The final pillar for recreating culture is hope. This is a pillar not only for the workplace culture but also for life.

> Building a positive culture on hope helps
> the existing team see how much potential
> we still have to reach.

If it's obvious that you, as the leader, aren't hopeful, forget about rallying the troops. Hopeful leaders create hopeful followers. And cultures. Negativity creates toxicity and drains motivation from anyone who comes within ten miles of it. Yuck.

Let's be real. Most of us who are stepping into something we didn't start will have to deal with a lot of negativity. You have to model what a hopeful attitude looks like. You have to model belief in something better.

## SIX PILLARS, ONE VISION

Creating new culture that is built on these life-giving pillars will get you going in the right direction.

The next big question?

Where are you going?

### QUICK QUESTIONS

1. Which of the four questions in this chapter needs to be answered now?

2. Where does toxic behavior exist currently, and what needs to be done to fix it?

# 11

## Vision Gets Major Points

*The only thing worse than being blind is having sight but no vision.*

—Helen Keller

For most of my life, I had heard about *The Hobbit* and *The Lord of the Rings* by J. R. R. Tolkien. I had just never read them. I actually didn't read much until college. Just kind of cruised my way from kindergarten through twelfth grade and then started enjoying to read. My problem was—and still is—that I can't focus on anything for longer than about four minutes.

Finally, in seminary, I decided to dive into these classic books. The first movie was coming out in about a year, and I really wanted to read *The Lord of the Rings* beforehand. To this day it's one of my favorite stories! After reading it for fun, I was asked to help with a seminary course on Tolkien's writings. That put me over the moon.

The saga has so many layers and plot lines. Unbelievable twists and turns. Heroes. Villains. Kings and warriors. It's the best.

The basic story begins in *The Fellowship of the Ring,* which introduces a fellowship made up of hobbits, men, a dwarf, an elf, and a wizard trying to destroy the one ring. The one ring was ancient, and if it fell into the wrong hands, evil hands, it could destroy all the good in the place called Middle-earth. You caught up?

Moving on, in the second volume, *The Two Towers,* the story picks up with a hobbit named Frodo who has to be the ring bearer because it belonged to him and his uncle Bilbo. Frodo and his closest friend, Sam, are on a journey to a place called Mordor and have been separated from their group. It's a crazy scene, but the two hobbits are completely lost in the Dead Marshes. They have no idea which way they've come or which way to go. They walk in circles. They make no progress. They have no compass or map. They can kind of see in the distance the mountains that are their destination, but when they try to go that way and navigate the rocks, they just continue walking in circles. All the colors are the same, the rocks look the same, and the paths look the same.

There are few characters who have a larger part in both *The Hobbit* (which is the prequel) and *The Lord of the Rings* than Gollum. He was once a hobbit-like creature, but Gollum found the one ring, and because of his obsession with it, the ring slowly destroyed him. It was his "precious."

Gollum makes a substantial reappearance in *The Two Towers* (even though we also see him in the first volume) because he's pursuing the hobbits to try to get the ring back. The twist at this part of the story is that the very creature who is trying to kill them ends up being the only one who can help them. He's the only one who knows the way out! He can see what they cannot.

## Vision Requires Sight

I love that quote from Helen Keller at the beginning of the chapter—"The only thing worse than being blind is having sight but no vision." How true. Vision in leadership may be the ultimate skill for any great leader. Have you ever experienced what the hobbits were feeling? Like everything you try just blends together and there's no clear path forward? Like going in circles keeps you on the crazy train?

Oftentimes in new assignments we shoot ideas and experience at problems and they just bounce off like arrows hitting metal. We don't realize it for a while, but we haven't looked up to figure out where we need to go! We can't tell people where we should go if we can't picture it ourselves.

What's a picture that's better than where we are now?

What does it look like to reach that goal?

What pieces have to fall in place to get us there?

All important questions. If we are to lead the way God wants us to lead, it's always going to involve vision for a future. Working with no idea where we are headed is like fishing on dry land. You have to fish where the fish are. Therefore, you have to see where to go!

I know we talked briefly about vision in chapter 4, but we need to dive deeply into it at this point because, without it, you really don't stand much of a chance of turning the tide in an organization or team you didn't start.

## THE LEGEND

When I was in seminary, I had the ridiculous honor of being discipled by one of the legendary American evangelists of the twentieth century, Dr. Robert Coleman. He was seventy-five years old when he came back to Gordon-Conwell Theological Seminary and, with his wife, moved back into campus family housing. I remember asking him why they had decided to live on campus. He said that because they had lived there when they started their marriage *fifty years* before, they wanted to finish it out in the same way!

Dr. Coleman was one of the greatest men I've ever known. And one of his attributes moved me most. When Dr. Coleman would talk about heaven, it was like he was actually ascending for a moment to the throne room, to a place where he could see Jesus face to face. His students would all sit and marvel at the joy and peace that came over his body as he described what he was seeing in his mind's eye. He would tear up every time as he spoke about the beauty and greatness he saw.

Dr. Coleman had vision for his future. It was all about that final destination. He knew where he was going and what was required on the journey. His prayer life, devotion, reading of the Word, loving students, and making disciples were all key elements to the journey toward heaven.

Have you ever been led in a way that moves you like that? Have you ever had a leader paint such a clear picture of the desired destination or outcome that you could almost feel it? That's your job now. When you are handed the keys to someone else's movement or organization, you will be forced to develop and share a vision, viscerally, of what the future looks like.

## THE KEYS TO GREAT VISION

Vision needs to be simple.

It needs to make sense.

It needs to be clear and hopeful.

Vision talks of a better day. A better product. A better world.

Vision oozes with best-case scenarios and explodes with passion.

So, how do we come up with it? Where do we go to find one? What if we're not great at vision?

Look. Some leaders do this more naturally than others, but that will never be an excuse. You have to cast vision on a regular basis. One of the reasons you have to speak vision until you're blue in the face is to train the new team how to say where they are going *and* keep their eyes on the prize. They need to know so clearly what the right path is that they could describe it in their sleep!

Here are four characteristics of great vision—vision that will move your organization to something greater.

### Compels

I'm going to shoot you straight. If your vision isn't compelling, it's not vision. If it's filled with numbers and trying to improve the past leader's metrics, it's not vision. It's a matter of answering some *why* questions:

> Why does what we do matter?
> Why does our work make a difference?
> Why do we need to show up every day and do
>    our best?
> Why should we turn this ship around?

Most of us grew up in families where we learned two important things about our future:

1. What we want to replicate
2. What we don't want to replicate

We saw things our families did that we loved. So we watched and developed game plans to do the same things for our kids when we became parents. But then there are the areas that caused pain. Areas that we struggled with while growing up. Consistent decisions that seemed to make no sense or lacked direction. And we made a vow to never do that to our families.

I understand the sentiment, but when it comes to setting a vision, I don't think the same applies. In our vocation, vision needs to be saturated with the positive stance of what we *are going to do*! There's nothing compelling about the negative areas we want to avoid.

Compelling vision is all about the privilege of doing what we get to do. The rabbit we get to chase. The people we will influence. The product that will change how an industry does business.

## Creates Curiosity

Compelling vision creates curiosity. When you develop and cast vision for a better tomorrow or a workplace that can change the community, you are building curiosity.

If your vision doesn't ignite curiosity, then it probably isn't going to capture people.

We are talking about the kind of curiosity that makes people better. Curiosity that helps us formulate new ideas to accomplish the vision. Curiosity that sparks change that will last. Curiosity that forces great questions.

You'll know that the vision is wimpy or too small if no one asks, "How can we do that?" Or if the vision requires no thinking or strategic ideas. Then it isn't big enough.

For example, if your vision is "to help kids improve their grades with after-school tutoring," that's for sure a noble and needed calling. But it's not super compelling, and it doesn't lead to curiosity. I move on after I read that and don't think about it again. What if it was a little more like this: "We believe that the next generation succeeds and moves us forward when they are equipped to solve problems. Our after-school training prepares them for the next stage with exceptional development of these skills"? I'm a little more curious now about how you'll do that, and the vision is compelling because I agree with the thesis that students need problem-solving skills.

As a follower of Jesus, I adhere to the simple idea that if a vision, plan, or goal isn't big enough that you need God's help, it probably isn't big enough. Let's go after visions that move our hearts and stir the hearts of our people. No more small, mediocre pictures. No more tiny visions that we can pull off without anyone's help. No more visions that don't stir our curiosity.

## Calibrates

A compelling vision that creates curiosity will also serve as a calibrating agent. A huge responsibility of our leadership in this season of transition is to help the team stay calibrated. If we don't know the tweaks required or the mechanisms we are using to accomplish the vision, we will be as lost as Frodo and Sam in the Dead Marshes.

If you attend a live musical and are there right before the show starts, you'll hear the orchestra tuning. It's really a calibration to make sure they are all in agreement. All tuned to the same note. Although the members play many different instruments, they all have to tune to the same note to make sure they will be playing in accord and not discord. When they are in tune, it's a beautiful thing. Have you ever heard a band or orchestra not in tune? Not calibrated correctly? It's awful. I can remember rehearsals at events I've produced where one of the band members started a song in the wrong key, while everyone else was on the same page. Ouch! It was horrible. I cringed and wanted to cover my ears. It was that bad.

---

Vision produces proper calibration.
It keeps us all tuned to the right key.

---

When you are inheriting a team that needs correction or taking over a group that's lost its way, a great obstacle to your vision can be a loss of focus. If focus is not strong, it won't keep the team in tune. If it's right, your team will know where they are going and won't stop until they accomplish the mission. Vision paints the picture that forces your team to get aligned in the same direction.

A few years ago, I went to visit my good friend Lysa TerKeurst, who leads Proverbs 31 Ministries. We talked at length about organizational leadership. Lysa models life-giving leadership as well as anyone I know. She's unreal. Her staff is focused, fun, and faithful to their vision.

As we discussed what we've learned as leaders, she shared a practice that has helped me keep the vision front and center. The idea had to do with their organizational structure. Lysa realized that if she, as the leader, was so entrenched in the day-to-day running of the ministry, she would lose sight of the big picture. She would be in danger of not giving proper attention to the next season of the ministry. So she created a new system that empowered staff members not only to do the tasks of their jobs but also to be the guardians of some aspect of the vision. She redrew their organizational chart, transforming it from a pyramid to a wheel—with each department getting an equal slice of the circle. Each department was the guardian of what made sense for that group.

The finance and operations team members were the guardians of reality, making sure the ministry didn't violate any HR regulations or budget parameters or 501(c)(3) nonprofit laws. The team working directly with her, which focused mainly on content and theology, were the guardians who helped oversee pacing and direction. She called them the Momentum team and said they were to focus on asking, "Where are we going, and how are we going to get there?" In my words, "How do we keep our focus on the bigger picture that we've been called to pursue?" The names she gave to each of the six parts of the wheel were Fuel, Reality, Momentum, Engagement, Words, and Ministry.

By tasking members of her various teams with being guardians of their part of the vision, Lysa is able to share the leadership load, empower her leaders, and enjoy reaching crucial goals together. She constantly allows this system to calibrate the engine that's going to get them to their vision. If there's an idea that doesn't accomplish that vision, the teams all speak into it from their areas of expertise, and together they know to cut it. No wasted time. No wasted resources.

Vision keeps us calibrated when it's compelling and fills us with curiosity.

## Course Corrects

As mentioned with Lysa's team, when a great vision is cast, it keeps us focused on the right target. There are great books about the danger of taking your eyes off the prize. We all do it. One such book is *Mission Drift* by Peter Greer and Chris Horst, which I recommend if you want to do a deeper dive into this subject.

I worked at overnight camps throughout my years in college. I'd still work at camps if I could! I can remember that our goal was to put big spiritual ideas into simple pictures for our kids to understand.

One of those illustrations that comes to mind was about a king. The king was planning to turn the throne over to one of his three sons. He couldn't decide who would serve the kingdom best, so he created a simple challenge for each of them to complete. Based on this he would choose his successor. The king stood on the opposite end of a huge field from the boys. The challenge was simple. Whoever could reach him in the shortest amount of time and with the fewest steps would win the challenge.

The first son was very zealous and took off with huge, jumping steps. He'd run and jump for a few strides while looking at the ground to avoid tripping and then look up to recalibrate and start off again. His path looked like a zigzag.

The second son saw the first zigzagging here and there. He was a little more detailed and came up with another plan. He would take small steps very close together. He would look up and then look down to take some steps. Back and forth. He avoided the dreaded zigzag but ended up with way too many steps.

The third son decided to keep it simple. Just as mariners focused on stars to guide them or cowboys used the sun for navigation, the third brother never took his eyes off his father. Instead of constantly looking up and down to make sure his feet were going the right way, he just stared straight at his king and walked to him. He won the crown.

I know this story may seem too simple and even a little childish, but I think that's often the easiest way to learn principles—and the point of the story helps us. We must not take our eyes off the vision that's lodged deep in our hearts. We have to be able to stay the course. Occasionally, we will have to course correct because we've lost sight of the vision. But a great vision will get us back on course in no time.

This is so important when you have just inherited influence by taking over something you didn't start. You will constantly need to keep your eyes on a North Star. For years, the team you've joined may not have been able to see through the clouds of poor leadership.

It's time for them to be led.

It's time for vision to stir them to great things.

It's time to show them the way.

## Quick Questions

1. What is one simple practice you can put in place this week to force yourself to be more curious?

2. Where does your team need calibrating toward the mission?

# 12

## 4D Modeling

*Leaders have the privilege and the responsibility of going first. The most powerful way that anybody can lead is by example.*

—Michael Hyatt

Most people don't know that my undergraduate degree from the University of Georgia is in technology education. I got my mechanical instincts from my dad. He's a legend with cars and anything that has parts. It just makes sense to him. I feel that way most of the time. I love working with my hands and building things because it's an outlet and it's fun to do.

Technology education was a new field of study that replaced industrial arts (shop class) in most schools in Georgia. Instead of learning to build furniture, students were taught how to do video production, photography, robotics, and computer-aided drafting (CAD). I'm serious when I tell you how much I loved every one of these skills. CAD quickly became one of my favorite programs, and I learned everything I could about it.

Did you ever try to draw your name or the name of your favorite team in block letters in middle school? You know—the letters with perspective and a 3D look? Yeah, those. Maybe it was the kid next to you who was always doodling, but you know what I'm talking about. Anyway, drawing in CAD is similar to that but way more complicated. We were drawing 3D pictures of engine parts, tools, and even full house elevations or pictures of what the house would look like from the street.

People have always been—and still are—amazed by 3D. When you watch HGTV and see the plan for a dream house, it's not a 2D drawing that you're looking at. Until they see a 3D image, it's difficult for many people to picture what the final product will look like. This type of drawing and imaging was developed entirely to help people really understand what something will look like when it's built or manufactured.

The concept of modeling isn't exclusive to designers and artists. Film producers continue to push the envelope with 3D movies that make it seem like the action is jumping off the screen. It's awesome. Some places like Disney even take it to 4D! Feeling the wind, being sprayed with water, and sniffing scents similar to what you are watching adds a fourth dimension so you actually feel like you're in the movie.

## GREAT LEADERS ARE GREAT MODELS

Let's be really clear, really early. I'm not talking about fashion models, although there are plenty of great leaders who look the part! I'm referring to leading the way. Showing the people you are leading a glimpse of the final product. The culture. The vision. So, as we are on the homestretch of this book, why does modeling matter? Consider this: *"Well done is better than well said."*

Benjamin Franklin said that.[1] I love it! In your inherited space, you've been saying it. Teaching it. Passionately conveying it. Now it's time to live it. The easiest way to get your team to buy into what you're preaching is to show them why your way is better than what they were doing. If you want your team to actually believe that what you're talking about can build a flourishing culture, you will have to show them. Show them how choosing trust will pay off in the long run. Demonstrate in meetings the posture trust has. Point out the moments when hard evaluations of products or ideas are needed. You go first. Put your ideas under the microscope. Model what it looks like to live out these lifegiving principles among your team.

Simple truth: if you don't, they won't. *Go first.*

## Integrity

I doubt I'll ever write a leadership book without including a section on integrity. If there is one way to lose the influence you've gained after stepping into something you didn't start, it's by your words and actions not lining up. I know leaders in ministry who can preach the paint off the walls on Sunday but don't live those messages Monday through Saturday. I know financial advisers who can tell you how to run your finances but don't buy into those same messages with their own finances.

Granted, we will never be perfect as leaders, but we should try to be our best. Especially when it affects the people around us: Our teams. Our friends. Our families. They deserve our best.

The reason we need to talk about integrity when it comes to modeling to your new team or group is that you are creating a foundational belief system. They are feeling you out just as you are feeling them out. They are waiting to see whether you really believe what you're selling them. Are you just reciting something you've read in a book, or do you actually believe what you are sharing? This group is deciding whether they want to be part of this moving forward. They are asking themselves whether you have what it takes. The jury is out, and the quickest way to get a negative verdict is to lack integrity.

The word I love to use when describing integrity is *consistency*. Integrity is at the heart of God, so obviously, integrity is at the heart of life-giving organizations. Ethical and moral behavior gives your company or ministry integrity. That's a standard.

What I'm talking about here is leadership integrity. Are you consistent as a leader? Can your team count on you to do what you say, or are they going to have to come in every day and wait to see which version of the new leader shows up?

---

We get the best out of our teams when they can trust who we say we are. We build that trust by behavior and decisions that model our beliefs.

---

## Character

Your new team is desperately curious about what you're made of. They are all wondering whether you have depth to your personality and character. How will you respond when things don't go your way? What will you do? Not only what will you do, but also how will you handle it? Will you exhibit the fruit of the Spirit in tough times, or will the real you come shining through? Your character will be on display when push comes to shove.

They will watch to discover both what you celebrate and what you allow.

I've said it before but it bears repeating: *leadership is not just what you do but also what you allow.*

What will you allow? Are you going to allow leaders to talk about others behind their backs? Will you let your team miss deadlines without accountability? Are you going to allow a team to behave or treat people below the standard you've promoted?

Character is the DNA of your leadership. Character shows what matters to you. Character takes a lifetime to build and minutes to lose. Be you. If you fake it early on, that will come out under stress, and it won't be pretty. If you don't know how to handle something, ask your team for help. If your team is looking to you as a counterbalance to the poor leadership they were just relieved of, they'll want to know how you are different . . . *really.*

## Relational Investment

A vital practice you have to model when you inherit influence is relational investment. How committed are you to the people now sitting around the circle with you? How approachable are you as their leader? Can you be found, or are you staying isolated?

From my very early days of leading, I've fought extremely hard to stay approachable. It didn't matter which seat I was sitting in; I wanted my message to be, "You can talk to me. No gossip about others, but other than that, let's talk." I wanted my office to be a comfortable place so anyone on the team felt free to come in, sit down, and catch up. I wanted every person on the team, all the way down to the interns, to know that I cared about them as people—not just what they did for me.

There may come a day when you have way too many people in the organization to have a schedule that is that free, but it's still all about posture. If every day you come in, go directly to your office, shut the door, and never come out, you will never show the team that you are part of the group. It's not fun to work for an isolated leader. It can result in a team floundering and not flourishing. If the only time you invest in your team is at all-staff meetings or when a group or individual is in trouble, then you're not investing.

---

If you're too busy to connect with your team,
no matter what position you have in the
organization, you're too busy.

---

I've got an easy way to invest relationally. I know you're going to think I'm crazy because of how simple this is. But here goes.

*Get to know the people around you well.* You might not be able to get to know everyone in the organization, but you can know those closest to you on the organizational chart. Learn their kids' names. Ask how their kids' sports are going. Find out how their spouses are doing at work. At the simplest, put their birthdays on your calendar and make sure you give them at least a card.

Spend five minutes a day walking around and seeing how the whole team's culture is doing. It might just be the greatest five minutes of your day.

People want to work with people they like. This does not mean you will lose your authority or the respect you so want and need. You actually gain the respect of others when you show that you are going to invest in them. Sometimes it might mean bringing someone along on a trip to show him how the business runs. Maybe you need to invite a young employee into the executive team meeting to let her be a fly on the wall and see how you are making decisions. Which leads me to my final thought.

## Decision-Making

I honestly think one of the most important skills to model for a team you stepped into is how to make good decisions. Decisions that are consistent with the newly articulated vision. Decisions that emphasize the value you put on organizational culture.

If you hide in your office and never come out, how will the team understand what good decisions look like? I understand that, as the leader, you need to make many decisions that are your responsibility. But everyone in your organization is constantly making decisions too. If you don't model this for them, how will they know how to make decisions that can further the vision rather than decisions that will crush the culture?

---

Model decision-making if you want
good decisions made.

---

When the team sees what healthy decision-making does for the betterment of your organization, they won't just take your word for it. They'll start to actually believe this is better and worthy of their time to learn. You've been teaching them; now show them.

Leader after leader has told me how hard it is to find great young talent and retain it. *Welp.* If you hand staffers responsibility with no authority, they won't learn everything they need to know. Especially how to make decisions. Try this: be real with these young leaders, and let them make some decisions—ones that won't crush the organization if they're wrong decisions. But any decision has to have some weight to it. Without weight, the young leaders don't get stronger. They need to learn what it feels like to make decisions.

## OFF TO THE RACES

There you go. *Just do all that!* Do you feel completely ready to take the keys? Probably not. But my prayer and hope for you is basic:

Love well.
Show the fruit.
Go first.
Lead well.
Give life.

Go get 'em, tiger.

You were called to this task. God is with you. Knowing that, you can lead well.

## QUICK QUESTIONS

1. What do you know you need to model from the very beginning?

2. Where do you want to focus the team's energy?

# Section 5

---

## REAL-LIFE LEADERS AND REAL-LIFE RESULTS

AS I PRAYED ABOUT AND PLANNED THIS BOOK, I KNEW I REALLY WANTED TO give you examples of leaders who've inherited influence and managed it well. Leaders who've brought life to some tough spots.

I'm so thankful for the following leaders and their willingness to talk at length about what they learned as they stepped into leading things they didn't start. Two of them have done so multiple times. One is now leading a world-renowned ministry that he's been at for thirty-plus years.

Each leader was at the top of my list in his or her respective space:

> An amazing coach
> A caring CEO
> A gentle ministry leader
> A successful pastor

I love when I get to introduce my friends to my friends. So, friends, meet Buzz, Cheryl, Jim, and Jimmy.

# 13

## Buzz Williams:
### Head Basketball Coach of Texas A&M

About six years ago, I met, via text, Coach Buzz Williams. At that time Buzz was the head basketball coach at Marquette University. He told me that he loved leadership and watched every leadership talk he could get his hands on. He wasn't joking. During the six years of our friendship, I've sent him books, videos, and talks to devour.

Coach has done some unbelievable leading at the highest level of college basketball. One of my favorite things about him is that his determination to build incredible men overrides his desire to see them win every game. Make no mistake—he, his staff, and his players are busting their tails to turn a program around and win championships. However, he's also coaching the hearts of his players.

Interviewing Buzz was a no-brainer for this book because he's leading a team he didn't build. His insight is invaluable, and I know you'll be better because of it.

*What's fun for me is that you're right in the middle of leading a team you didn't recruit. So I feel like this concept of getting people on board with a new leader is a very real thing for you presently. Give us just a little context of a couple of times you've had to step into inherited spaces.*

It's been a little different each time. This is my fourth time being named head coach at an institution. My first, at the University of New Orleans, was the basketball season immediately following Hurricane Katrina. It was my first opportunity to be a head coach, and New Orleans was in really rough shape six months after Hurricane Katrina. So keeping the doors open to the institution was incredibly hard. Having some level of athletic team was almost impossible. They ended up going to Division III and then eventually came back to Division I.

Next, I was an assistant for seven months at Marquette prior to being the head coach. I should not have gotten the head job there when I did. A lot of "real" coaches tried to get it. Marquette was a completely different situation in that it's a top-twenty basketball job year in and year out. And there were returning players on the roster at Marquette who would later be in the NBA.

After Marquette, I went to a completely different scenario at Virginia Tech. Virginia Tech had finished in last place three consecutive years in the ACC, which at that time I think was probably the best basketball conference in the country. And we proceeded in year number one to finish in last place. So, the worst job at that time in the best league. I was there for five years.

Currently, we are a little over two hundred days in at Texas A&M. Off-and-on success throughout the history of the program. Very little sustainability. The one stretch of time when there was sustainability, I was an assistant for a portion of that, which I think led to some degree to my opportunity to return as the head coach. The job had been open a few times since I had left, and I had turned the job down each time. Felt like this was the right time to try. So, each coaching scenario has been different.

*What's crazy is that the idea of leading something you didn't start is pretty fresh for you right now! What are a couple of key leadership lessons you've learned after doing this a few times—starting from day one, when you've come into a team you didn't recruit with players who didn't sign up for you? They signed up for a different coach and a different program. What leadership principles have you tried to implement?*

I follow, obviously, a lot of basketball stuff. One thing I've tried to do throughout my career is study guys like you who run Catalyst and then leave. Pastors who pastor a church and then leave. I try to study it in every type of space because I think there are transferrable things that are important.

In college athletics, because of the exposure, because of the money, you sometimes see people making decisions who maybe haven't earned the right to make those decisions, because they were thrown into the fire and haven't done it before. So, I study a lot of that in football, particularly in the NFL and in college.

I was talking to an athletic director last week who just made a football hire. And I was telling the athletic director, "If you could, let's break the cycle of having the new football coach parade around to all the donors and all the boosters before giving him an opportunity to diagnose what he has. Let the new coach invest in and spend time with the kids who are there before trying to sign more, and allow him time to think about what would best allow him to get the right start before hiring a staff."

I think one of the things that I tried to do better this time than ever before is saying no to more things in my first hundred days so I could spend as much time as the calendar would allow on campus, meeting people but also just spending time with our players. Because everybody thinks of the change in relation to me. And it is my family. It is the staff I hire. It is their families. But it's also a distinct change for those kids. It's a distinct change for the kids who are here. It's a distinct change for the kids who had signed with the previous staff to come here and found themselves in limbo in the spring of their senior year of high school. And I think I tried to be more intentional. Prior to my hiring, Texas A&M had signed four players who were scheduled to be on the team this year, and I gave all four their release.

As a coach, I don't know whether that's the right thing to do right away, but it was the right thing to do from my heart because I did not feel convinced that those kids believed this was the right place. Not that it was anything against me, but as a coach you don't want to be held hostage in any sort of way if you're trying to build something that's sustainable. And if you're not going to feel held hostage, you have to invest time with the people who are already a part of the program prior to your arrival so you can better understand their hopes, their dreams, their fears, their goals. And I tried to be more conscious of that this time maybe than ever before.

*There's definitely two ways to do this, right? With the mentality that there's a new sheriff in town and this is how we do it and you're either on board or off. Or you come in with a little bit more gentleness, a little bit more kindness. It sounds like patience was a big play for you in this. Talk about patience in this conversation.*

I become overwhelmed with the confusion that comes from leadership, and there's so much chaos when you take a job—chaos personally, chaos professionally. I think there's emotional chaos too.

At Virginia Tech, we were playing in the Sweet 16 in DC and got beat by Duke at the buzzer on a Saturday. And on Wednesday night, I'm on a plane to attend a press conference on Thursday. I think it takes time to process that.

But it's hard to lead those who don't understand what you're teaching and coaching to become those who do. It takes time to help them, nurture them, develop them, and grow them into people who do understand. I'm not a patient person in some regards. I'm an incredibly patient person in other regards. This is my thirteenth consecutive year as a Power Five head coach at three different institutions. And one thing I've learned is that sometimes my timetable was based on other people's opinions. Sometimes my timetable was dependent on the administration that hired me. Sometimes it was dependent on Twitter or what people's expectations were.

The athletic director who hired me here at Texas A&M left twelve days later, and his position was open for the next seventy days. And then the guy who replaced him obviously had his own leadership style.

*Something I've admired about you, Coach, from the day we met is that Coach Buzz Williams is the same. You do different things, but who you are as a man and how you carry yourself moves right into all these spaces. I think one of the greatest principles for stepping onto an inherited platform is to be your truest self. How have you been able to do that when all that pressure around you says, "I need you to do this; I need you to do that"?*

It's so hard. Thanks for your kind words. I think that's a book; that question—"How do you stay your truest self?"—and the answers are a book. Because everybody defines success in a different way and everyone has different thoughts on what is important here on earth and what is important eternally.

The one thing I've learned as I've gotten older, though, is the word *time*—sustainable time—has to be included in whatever your definition of success is. Did the team do it in one year? Did they do it in one season? Did they do it for two seasons? Did they do it over a long period of time? There's something in each person's definition, in my opinion, that has to include the word *time*.

And I wonder if, no matter which players are on our roster, no matter if they're supposedly good or if they were ranked or if they weren't ranked or if they're not good or if it was the old coach who recruited them or if it was the new coach and they're young—whatever justifications you come up with (and you can almost do the same thing with the staff you hire)—I wonder if I can be the same before we have success, while we are experiencing success (if there is any), and after we have success. I wonder if, whatever the results are, they will not change me. And I think that's incredibly difficult. I think you have to be very disciplined in what you allow your eyes to see and what you allow your ears to hear and what you put in your heart.

As a young person, I had heard people say how lonely leadership is. And I never really understood how a person could be lonely in that position. But I do feel the loneliness. I don't feel that way in a "pity me" way. I feel that being lonely is the best way for me to lead because I have to be really careful about what is in my sphere. Because, as a leader, I think your most important responsibility is to figuratively feed those you're leading. And in order to consistently feed those people, you have to have a diet of your own.

**You have to give them something.**

That's right. And your diet is going to determine the nutrients you're giving to those you're leading. And as I've progressed, the number of people in my tribe continues to grow because I'm developing even better leaders, and it's not just who's on my team anymore. It's who's been on my team. They may not be playing or on my staff, but they're still a part of my team. And because I have such a chaotic mind, I've got to be really, really careful with what I allow in my brain and what I allow in my soul. Because I can't be the same in how I handle success and failure unless I have consistency in what I'm figuratively eating.

And I think, just to expand a little bit more, when you walk into a situation that's not necessarily all your own doing, you have to have some level of liberation. I'm not going to use this as an excuse. I am going to give credit where credit is due and not make it seem as though

I did something, and I'm going to make sure that all the decisions I make not only fit the short-term objective but also bleed into the long-term goals.

I think a lot of coaches do things in the short term to put a Band-Aid on a wound, but in the long term those short-term decisions—those short-term Band-Aids—do not do the job, and then they look back later and think, *I shouldn't have put those Band-Aids on because that led to some level of stagnation in what I was trying to grow.* Yet in a game they think, *Hey, let's just forget that's one of our principles. Let's just try to win this game, and we'll deal with that Band-Aid later.*

I just don't know if there's sustainability in that. I think that's where a lot of leaders struggle: Who's in your sphere and what are you feeding yourself? And then how are you regurgitating that to those you're leading? And does that all make sense to them in relation to what you're doing in the short term? How does that feed the long term?

*That tends to be the tension for us as leaders: we've got owners; we've got shareholders; we've got elder boards; we've got donors to the university. They want instant results, but you know, Coach, that you can't build a program like that. One of the things I wrote about in The Life-Giving Leader is that when life flows, influence grows. And that's how your influence has continued to grow— you've poured life into people. But for you—and you've been very open about this—faith has been a vital part of that life that you've poured into others. How has that helped you navigate as you walk into some of these spaces?*

We played a really bad team last night. We haven't won a game in almost a month. And I feel convicted almost hourly by these questions you and I could talk about all day long. And maybe you wrote this, or maybe somebody else wrote it: "When you breathe in, say, 'Jesus, You can,' and when you breathe out, say, 'I can't.'"

I've realized that I have been blessed way more than I deserve. I used to think those blessings were things that made me look at scoreboards—what I thought mattered. And now I realize those things don't matter. And what I've realized is maybe those blessings really were not things but responsibilities. To be a steward of those blessings is to help those I'm leading. Whether we win or lose, I can still be a steward of what I think is going to matter long term. And the experiences of the young men while a part of our program will make them better not only as players but also as people. And because of all that, I seem to coach less basketball.

I still like it because of how big the job has become today. There's less ball and a lot more other stuff. The best twenty-first-century leaders, whether basketball coaches or not, are the ones who are really good at mind management. Managing their own minds and also helping others manage theirs. The world is just going so fast. Particularly in what I do, the players are nineteen to twenty-two years old, and they're overwhelmed and inundated with tweets and direct messages and social media. You've got to help them learn to manage their minds through all that. But you can't help them manage it if you can't manage it yourself.

*One of the things I have loved is that you've evolved as you've grown as a coach, because you're handing more coaching to your assistant coaches. One of your coaches has become a close friend, and I really care about him and enjoy watching him step into that space. He's getting to coach the things you love, and you've stepped into a different season, which is coaching the whole thing. Talk about vision, especially considering you're in a tough spot right now. You're sitting here, and everybody thinks, Oh, he's got a great gig. No, you really have a lot going on. How does vision stay in your character and your heart and your mind, and how is that spilling over as you transition a program?*

That's the deal. I can draw up an out-of-bounds play. I know what's supposed to be happening tactically. I have passed bits and pieces of that on because I think that's the next right step for those I've passed it on to. I've kind of already been through that. Doesn't mean that I have to completely release it, but if I give them ownership, they feel like they're growing. And I think when our kids see that their coaches have ownership, now they understand how to be a better teammate. I think there's a lot of lessons to it.

And I think opposition—whatever the opposition is; everybody has different opposition—can have a refining effect on vision. Through all the opposition you go through as a leader, your vision should be growing. #getbetter.

If the things that I'm doing today are the same things I was doing in 2010, then I haven't lived by my mantra of #getbetter. Along the path of #getbetter, there's going to be opposition, and that opposition, if you're studying it, if you're paying attention to it, if you're thinking about it, should refine your vision. Maybe it includes winning every game, but maybe that vision is something *above* winning every game. You hope that it includes winning games, but are you okay if your vision says that even if you don't win games, you're still going to do right? I think that's what's hard.

There's a lot going on two hundred days into my tenure here, and I have to be really careful when it comes to my vision. Yesterday before our game, I was showing film clips to my guys of something that happened in college basketball, and it wasn't for our game yesterday. It was potentially for some game three years from now. As I commentated on the clip, I said, "Guys, I'm not showing you this for today. If it happens today, I'll be glad it worked out, but I'm showing you this because I know where we're going and I know how we're going to get there and I know the steps it takes and this is an important lesson. I can't keep it in a file and show it when it's time to take that step. Because then it will have lost its essence of time. This happened yesterday. I want you to watch it. I'm going to comment on it. We're going to pause it twenty-nine thousand times, and we're going to work through all of this."

Crazy, ironic, or not ironic—maybe sovereign—that scenario that I had shown my guys yesterday morning played out almost exactly the same last night. I think you can't have vision if you live by your seat. You have to have vision by your feet. You've got to live by your feet. Where are your feet taking you?

Tom Landry was one of my favorite coaches as a kid, and he would always be at the training camp in Thousand Oaks, California. He would be up in the tower, kind of watching. And then Jerry Jones buys the team, fires Tom Landry, and it's like, *What's going on?* And he hires Jimmy Johnson. Jimmy Johnson is out there running drills.

You can't cast vision by your seat. You have to do it by your feet, and you have to be ahead of those you're leading so they know, *Yeah, that's the path we're supposed to take.*

# 14

## CHERYL BACHELDER:
### Former CEO of Popeyes

WHEN I STARTED THINKING ABOUT LEADERS I KNEW WHO HAD INHERITED huge opportunities and big-time platforms, Cheryl Bachelder was at the top of my list. She is one of the best leaders I know, and she is able to articulate the principles and leadership values she learned while leading a massive company.

In this last section, I chose to feature leaders from different careers to show how many principles work across the board. Whether you're in business, ministry, nonprofit work, or even coaching, the principles of leadership are applicable.

This matters. The people you connect to and lead matter. Cheryl has led in many places, but when she inherited Popeyes fast-food empire, she was faced with perhaps the biggest challenge of her professional career. Her faith and leadership are inspiring. I'll let her tell you more about it.

*To begin, here's Cheryl giving you a little more detail about her experience.*

My entire career has been in large corporations. So, as I thought about your thesis in this book, every job I've ever had was inherited. I've never been an entrepreneur. I've never done a start-up, and I like the word *inherited* because every new job or new role you take in a corporation is a new assignment. The entity or the enterprise and the people are always already there—always. And the other thing that I think is relevant is that, in corporate life, most assignments don't last very long. A year or two is a long assignment in a corporation.

I joined a very large company straight out of college called Procter & Gamble (P&G). It was one of the best training companies in brand management, and that was my desired field, so I went there when I graduated. From there, I went to Gillette, a company that P&G later bought. Gillette was also famous for strong brands.

I then made a big shift from packaged goods into food, going to Nabisco. I was there for nine years through a lot of change and transition—many, many assignments at Nabisco. And then I leveraged all that experience to make a shift into food franchising. I went to Domino's Pizza. I learned the business from the founder, Tom Monaghan. Best teacher of that industry I could have had, and that really set up the rest of my career, which was in restaurant franchising.

I went from Domino's to KFC to Popeyes. Each one of those was a brand that had once been thriving but had lost its way and had to be brought back on track, so to speak. So, turnarounds and new assignments are kind of the story of my whole career.

*This is hard stuff, isn't it?*

There were a number of times when I said, "Now, what was I thinking?"

*Yes, because at times you would want to inherit something that was actually cruising and doing well. That would be a fun experience.*

Well, you have to go with your personality, and I actually would find cruising boring. I'm all about challenge and growth and learning something new—to try something and innovate. I'm just wired for the complex messes, and corporations have quite a few of those.

*Let's say you just got a new inherited opportunity, one that you're going to head into in a few weeks. You've done some research, and you know what you're getting into. What are a few leadership thoughts you have going in, some things you put in your tool belt to be ready to lead this new team, this new group, this new platform?*

The first thing that I always remind myself, because it's not a natural instinct, is to listen first. You always assume you know the situation, and you just can't possibly know the situation. So, at Popeyes, I did a seven-city listening tour. I listened to franchise owners, I listened to restaurant general managers, and I listened to customers in every city. I just wrote down what they said. I didn't try to put a spin on it.

When I got back, I knew so much more about the reality of the situation and what needed to be done. There's a line that says, "The answers are in the room." They really are if you listen for them. So, listen first.

The second thing, after you've listened, is to develop a coherent road map for your team. I use the phrase *road map* because people have to know where you want them to go, where they need to focus, what the few vital things are that they need to work on often. They are not the things they're working on right now.

At Popeyes, I found the team working on 128 active projects, and the business had been declining for seven years. You might conclude that none of those projects were helping very much. So, which seven projects do you choose? Pick a number, but something fewer than ten. Which projects or directions do you want them to focus on? Most leaders don't spend enough time refining and narrowing the expectations. They let the organization continue to just kind of stumble along on all the different things, and it doesn't create outcomes.

Then the third thing is to make time for these people you've been asked to lead. Most leaders grossly underestimate the time it takes to lead people, and they don't put it on their calendars and do it. I eventually directed my team to spend a third of their week coaching their direct reports, and they panicked when I said that. "Where is that third going to come from?" they asked. And I just said, "How are you going to get all this done if you don't?" It's the most important investment you make.

*I love the process you outlined. I think so many people move into new roles and new teams and they want to be the new boss. They want to come with all the ideas. But you and I both know that when you're stepping into roles that already existed, you can't do that. You've got to get the team rallied around who you are as a leader. So, how do you do that? How do you get a team that you didn't recruit on board with who you are as a leader and where you want to go?*

Well, first a tactical thing and then maybe a broader view. My HR director taught me to do what she called a manager assimilation meeting.

It's the first meeting you have with the team, where you spend some time getting to know one another. You getting to know them and, just as important, them getting to know you—being able to ask their questions, being able to ask you what your expectations are, what your values are, what your style is, what they can do that will make you happy.

If you don't dedicate any time to getting to know them and allowing your team to get to know you in a very transparent, open way, it will take a very long time for them to truly understand you and who you are. So, tactically, spend some time on it.

The second thing that comes to mind is the criteria for being a great boss who engages her team quickly and performs her best. This is a very well-researched and documented question. It's just hardly ever well done.

I've done a lot of study on the Gallup organization's work around human engagement, and they have this test called the $Q^{12}$ survey that basically lets employees rate their bosses. So, this is not rocket science. The research has been around for my whole career, and the whole time they've been measuring this, fewer than 20 percent of all workers in America are highly engaged in their work. That means we have lots of lousy bosses, just lots. If you want to be a great boss, first think about one you had and what he did for you and ask yourself, *Am I going to do those things for others?*

The twelve questions are as follows:

1. Do you know what is expected of you at work?
2. Do you have the materials and equipment to do your work right?
3. At work, do you have the opportunity to do what you do best every day?
4. In the last seven days, have you received recognition or praise for doing good work?
5. Does your supervisor, or someone at work, seem to care about you as a person?
6. Is there someone at work who encourages your development?

7.  At work, do your opinions seem to count?
8.  Does the mission/purpose of your company make you feel your job is important?
9.  Are your associates (fellow employees) committed to doing quality work?
10. Do you have a best friend at work?
11. In the last six months, has someone at work talked to you about your progress?
12. In the last year, have you had opportunities to learn and grow?[1]

That's what you want from your boss. That's what I want from my boss. So, the only question is, Are you going to be this kind of leader for the people who have been entrusted to your care, or are you going to be a lousy boss? This is a lot of hard work for a boss, by the way. Everybody thinks the work is done by the followers. At least half the work's done by the boss. So, as the boss, are you going to invest in those things that create good followers, happy followers, engaged people? Those are the things people want from you, period.

*I've said a lot of times that leadership's not as hard as people make it out to be. If you care for people, you're probably going to do okay.*

Caring for people, though, is an intentional act. Don't miss this point. It's a planned act. In my career, I have never met anyone who's spent a whole hour preparing a performance review for a team member. That's bad.

That means we don't really care. That means it's lip service. Right? And then you ask the follower, and she says, "Oh yeah, I've had one of those feedback sessions, and you told me what was wrong with me for fifty-five minutes and thanked and praised me for five. What did I take from that? I'm a schmuck in your worldview."

We really just lie to ourselves that we're investing enough time in giving our people this kind of leadership. It takes time. You have to prepare. You have to be intentional. That's what caring is. Caring is action. It's not thinking about it.

*So, let's say you've moved in, you've done these things, and yet the team is still not getting it. Obviously, you have to be patient. What do you do when a team member just doesn't seem to be on board with you as a leader? How long do you coach him before you make a change? What does that look like in your mind?*

The first thing is to make sure you've diagnosed the situation correctly. That is, again, a listening thing. First asking him, "What is holding back your performance? What are your roadblocks? What are the trouble spots?" Because you might have diagnosed it incorrectly.

I remember vividly a situation where a high performer became a poor performer, and I couldn't figure out why. And when I asked gently and appropriately, this person told me she had significant problems going on at home, and it completely reframed my understanding of what was realistic to ask for. Had I not asked, I might've been quite tough and demanding and said, "Get back on track. You are a high performer!"

But knowing what I found out, I said, "Oh my goodness." The way to get this high-performance person back on track was by supporting her during this difficult time. What did she need, and how quickly did she think she could get back on track?

The interesting thing about that approach is, if you actually know what the problem is, you will build tremendous loyalty from people, who will say, "Oh my goodness, she took the time to find out, and therefore, she cares. And therefore, I will do whatever it takes to perform."

*So, how does patience play into this conversation? How long do you wait, and how long do you honor the past? In the different spaces you stepped into, how did patience play into your leadership?*

I think patience is essential because bringing out the best in people is not a fast process but it is a powerful path to performance. Our culture wants everything to be quick. Quick and efficient. But you cannot be quick and efficient with people. My favorite way to challenge people on this is to say, "Think about the last time your boss was quick with you. How'd that feel?" And it doesn't take you a nanosecond to say, "It did not feel good. It was dismissive. It conveyed I wasn't important. It conveyed that something else was more important to my boss than my problem, my work, me, and it did not motivate me to do my best."

I had this fun little exercise. I had a very efficient leader on my team who had a strict calendar, and when he was done talking to you, it was over. So the next time I coached him, I got out my watch, laid it on the table, and did the same to him. And he said, "What are you doing?" I said, "I'm being you. How does it feel?" And he said, "It feels terrible." I said, "Okay, let's change it."

Because being efficient does not convey care. Firm boundaries on time don't either. I mean, I'm a little sloppy with my calendar because human beings don't work on a clock, right? If I just got to the root cause of an issue with a person, I've got to stay in it and work through it, even if it means I'll be late to the next meeting.

So, patience, appropriate time with people, and understanding that there's nothing efficient about humans—those are essential to bringing out great performance. It's not patience with poor performance. No. It's patience with a person to get to high performance.

*Cheryl, there's something I've always respected about you, and I really tried to take the same approach when I went to Catalyst. In your book, Dare to Serve, you have a concept of coming in to serve, not to be served. Why is that a life message for you? Why is it so important to come from a posture of serving?*

Leadership is stewardship, responsibility, and a worldview. So, it's an opportunity I've been given to serve a group of people over a period of time, and my central premise is it's about that enterprise and those people, not about me. It's the mindset that I bring. And, by the way, no one, including me, is good at serving every day. That's like saying "I'm humble." Right? As soon as you say it, you're not, and serving is the same way.

I aspire to serve these people who have been entrusted to my care, but it's a constant battle to overcome self-interest and make them the priority. For instance, I may be tired and rushed today. How do I stop, collect myself, make these people a priority, and be available to them? That's work. You've got to get through that—the barriers in your own brain—to serve people.

For example, I got up this morning and made breakfast for my husband. I had to get over the fact that I didn't want to make breakfast and do it for the reason of helping another person. So, it's that whole message of thinking of others more than yourself. I often tell my high achievers, "You want to do something really hard? Think of others more than yourself. That'll take the rest of your life to work on." It's a really fun thing to do with ambitious, driven people because they want a challenge. They just want to take the hill. I say, "Oh, take that hill of serving others. That hill's really hard."

**Yeah. It's messy, too, isn't it?**

It's a hard, messy, daily effort. Yeah. That's climbing a volcano, right? It's take one step, slide back two.

*Cheryl, you mentioned earlier that many of these places where you stepped in—actually, most of them—had been in decline or weren't up and to the right. Culture plays a huge part in that. What were a couple of keys for you when you went into these situations, specifically when it came to culture? What were you thinking about? What were you doing to shift the culture in those organizations?*

I think the key to culture is the same as the key to your business plan, and that's clarity of expectations. For me, culture is establishing the principles that you want to guide all the people's behavior. Because if they're not well defined, then you're going to have a hard time holding people to them and seeing the impact on performance.

At Popeyes, as an example, we chose six principles. We then explained the principles: what they meant and what behaviors were expected. And then we modeled them, we monitored them, and we corrected behavior. I'll give you a simple example. The first one was passion, and passion's kind of a strange principle. You expect passion. Well, what we actually were saying was that we expected respect for passion because we were leading entrepreneurs, and entrepreneurs are far more passionate than they are fact based, right? They have lots of opinions and very few facts. But you have to respect that because they have all their money in the business and you invest nothing. That's how the franchise model works. They put everything on the line. You've got to respect that, and you've got to listen to their passionate plea and assume there's truth somewhere in it rather than berating them all the time for not having facts. So, respect for passion was guideline number one, and it really was a way to teach respect for our franchise owners.

*I really like that, and it helps give language. It puts flesh and skin on what we're going to be about, doesn't it?*

It does, and it allows you to repeatedly say to your team, "Oh, I understand that you're angry. I understand that you're impatient with the franchise owner, but let's go back to the beginning. Let's think about what he has invested and what you have invested. Let's respect his passion. He's in this for the long term. All his money, his life, and his family are on the line. This is a sweat equity investment. Let's give him respect."

*Do you have an example of a time when you went in and it didn't go well? A time when you said, "Gosh, that was harder than I expected, and I didn't handle it great"?*

Well, I've talked about this publicly many times, but I got fired from my leadership role at KFC, and there's nothing like that to teach you a lesson. I often say, "We don't learn much from our successes, but, boy, a good failure will whack you upside the head."

I actually hadn't thought about this error. I was crystal clear on the business direction and the principles of how I wanted to work with my team. I chose my team well. What I failed to do was get aligned with my boss's expectations. What I was planning to do was not aligned with his ideas, and that's how you get fired—being out of sync with your leader or your board or whomever you work for.

I was thinking about what I was going to do as a leader and did not listen carefully. I never spent the time getting aligned with my boss on what he needed me to do, when he wanted it completed, and how he would define success. Obviously, I didn't meet that in his time frame. Confident leaders often rush into battle without giving these things consideration.

*Wow, that's hard but true. Even when a pastor goes to a church and thinks, I'm the lead pastor, so I call the shots! Well, no, you have an elder board. You have these groups of people who have been here for a while, and that's why listening to them and getting aligned with them is important. It goes back to vision a little bit, too, right? What is the vision for where we're going? I know culture and vision are different for me. Culture is those expectations about behavior. It is that understanding of who we're going to be and how we're going to act. It's usually more around character. Vision is about where we're going and how we're going to get there. How have you seen vision play an important role in inheriting influence?*

Before we leave that thought about boards and elders, there is no leader on the planet who doesn't have a boss except God. And for faith-filled people, it's God. People often are quite enamored with CEOs because they're the ultimate. The buck stops there. They're the boss. Those people completely forget that there are shareholders and a board. CEOs get fired every two and a half years on average, so it is the toughest subordinate role—but nobody ever thinks about that.

Vision's a fancy word for "clarity of expectations," for asking, "Where are we going?"

*And your road map?*

The reason I call it a road map is that I have a really good friend, a thirty-year colleague, who always uses this analogy. He says, "Listen. You're taking the people on a family vacation, and they need to know what to pack. Are you going to the beach or to the mountains? It makes a difference."

So, you absolutely owe it to the people to define the destination clearly and explain what to bring, how best to contribute, and what their roles are. Break it down. Vision is an end to work toward, but you also break it down to "Okay, now that we know we're going to the beach, bring the surfboard, bring the suntan oil." There's a list of what you take to the beach. There's a list of skills you need at the beach that you don't need in the mountains. You really wrestle through those details in your vision so that the people can best contribute.

I'm terrible at sports, so I use zero sports analogies, but I really do like mountaineering as an example of a team sport because of all the preparation, all the planning, all the anticipation. We are going to climb that mountain. Here's what you're going to bring; here's how you're going to prepare; here's how we're going to keep from dying on the mountain. It's just a really good analogy for what good visionary leadership looks like. And what an accomplishment if you get a team of ten people to the top of Everest and nobody died—you're a superhero! As a leader, it is a team sport; it isn't solo.

*It doesn't matter how successful we are or how much credibility we have as leaders—we're all insecure in different ways, and we've got some fears. What were some of your fears when you walked into a situation that was declining or tough or when you were just inheriting a new space?*

First, fear is always about time. Will there be enough time? Are the expectations about time aligned? Does the board think a three-year turnaround will work, or are they thinking three months? Are the people capable of changing fast enough, considering how behaviors and skills are pretty deeply embedded in an organization? So, time is what I fear most—knowing what to do and running out of time . . . and it happens all the time.

*It's those unwritten expectations, isn't it?*

Yeah, and it's hard to be realistic about time. An example I would give is that, in restaurant land, you have many, many competitors. You may be working on the right thing, but if you don't get it done fast enough, it won't be a competitive advantage. You won't grow market share, and you'll be further down the decline path.

So, getting important things done in a timely fashion is something you should hear about from your team's performance and it's something you should know. Having a sense of urgency about these things is so important.

I'm currently working on my goals, like all people do on January 1, and time is not a replaceable resource. You get one shot at time, so understanding that can evoke fear.

*I agree with that. If we had a room full of leaders who were all stepping into inherited positions, what's one piece of advice you'd give? What's one thing you would encourage them to just think about and be prepared to do?*

I think I would really home in on the word *curiosity*. The fastest way to come up to speed in any circumstance is to ask questions, listen to the answers, and weave a much richer understanding of the situation. Get your facts; get your insights; talk to all your constituents. Curiosity is the fastest path to a plan that can have impact. I mean, you can act fast, but if you're acting on the wrong things, you won't have impact.

*Curiosity is really important when we want to make changes and make them quickly but we don't know the history of what we're stepping into. There's homework required for that, right? Because even when you celebrate stuff, you must celebrate correctly. If you celebrate the wrong things, then you're going to create a vision or a culture that says, I'm going to allow this. This is a great thing.*

I'll give you a quick example. When I joined Popeyes, there was an article in the restaurant trade magazine that said we were ranked nearly the slowest quick-service restaurant chain in the United States. We were ninety-eight out of one hundred. So we asked a question: Why? We hadn't been measuring the speed of our drive-through. There were no tools in the restaurant to measure this—nobody knew how slow we were. The industry standard was 90 to 120 seconds per customer at the drive-through window, and when we put the timer up over the drive-through, it said 400. So we asked another question: If we had a timer, we would know our speed, and if we knew, we could do something about it, right? We had to drive it steadily down to the industry standard. Curiosity led to some obvious solutions.

*One last question, and I think this is just ingrained in me from seven years of leading at Catalyst and loving emerging leaders and next-generation leaders: What's the one leadership lesson you would tell yourself back when you were in your early twenties—something that you now look back and say, "Gosh, I wish I'd known this lesson"?*

There's just one. It's Philippians 2:3, which tells us to count others as more significant than ourselves. And the reason I say that to young leaders is that it's all about our significance. We're trying to become something; we're building a résumé; we want to be known; we want to have an impact; we're missional. I love all that stuff about humans— our desire to change the world. It's a beautiful thing. But consider others more significant than yourself, and see how that changes the impact you make.

Today, now that I'm old and wise, I want to have an impact on my grandchildren, but you can argue that when I was twenty-eight and leading a team of ten, I should've been thinking just as intentionally about the impact I wanted to have on those folks so that they might be more effective, they might grow, they might learn. That's the real legacy.

# 15

===

# JIM DALY:
## President of Focus on the Family

ONE OF THE THEMES I WANTED TO EMPHASIZE IN THIS BOOK WAS NOT ONLY the challenges for leaders who take over something they didn't start but also, in some situations, the reality that the public will evaluate the leaders' performance.

Jim Daly serves as a perfect case study for this because he took over at Focus on the Family for the organization's founder, Dr. James Dobson. Whether you agree or disagree with the efforts of Focus or even with Dr. Dobson, this organization has an amazing record as a large ministry that has fought to serve kids and families using Bible studies, radio broadcasts, and many other services, initiatives, and products.

The mission of Focus on the Family is clear: to cooperate with the Holy Spirit in sharing the gospel of Jesus Christ with as many people as possible by nurturing and defending the God-ordained institution of the family and promoting biblical truths worldwide.

One of the other reasons I wanted to interview Jim for this book was that he was promoted from inside of the organization. Sometimes taking over is not coming from the outside to turn it around, as Cheryl Bachelder did, but growing up in the organization and then being handed the keys.

Jim exudes humility and grace. His heart is always to help others see God, and I'm honored to share with you some of what he's learned.

*Here are Jim's words about his journey to the top seat.*

I came from the business community. I got my MBA, and I worked for International Paper. A friend of mine had moved from Campus Crusade for Christ to Focus on the Family. He called me and said, "Hey, there's a position opening at Focus, and I think you'd be really well suited for it." I said okay, but I wasn't that intrigued by the opportunity. It was as if I were having an early midlife crisis, asking myself, *Is my current career meaningful?* I talked to my wife, Jean, about it, and she encouraged me to seek God's heart. She added, "I trust your judgment, and I'm with you no matter what decision you make," which built up my confidence. I kind of ignored the idea and thought, *If God wants me to make a change, He'll work it out.* Well, a promotion came through a few months later, and my friend called me again the very same day, asking if I was ready to consider this Focus position. I had three days to decide. I interviewed and accepted the offer from Focus in a forty-eight-hour time frame. I took one-third the salary I had been making! Jean was fine with it. What is so funny is that Jean and I thought we would do this for two or three years—kind of give our contribution to the Lord—and then we'd get back to making money and doing the things we needed to do to buy a house and start our family.

And it is just funny because our plans tend to be very different from what God has planned for us. That's probably lesson one. Just be open handed with where God wants to lead you. So, that's how I ended up at Focus. I had no clue what the Lord was going to do over the next thirty years. It has included a variety of assignments at Focus.

Over a five-year period, I became vice president of marketing, vice president of international, and vice president of public affairs. I was made the chief operating officer, and then in February 2005, I was made president. I had no clue. I really was just trying to do my best every day. I wasn't a corporate climber. I didn't feel like that. But I think being prepared and trying to do the best I could do with the gifts God had given me caught Doc's [Dr. James Dobson's] attention and also the board's attention. So, I was very honored when they asked me to step into the role, although also very fearful at the time.

*One of the things that's interesting, Jim, is that, of the people I've interviewed, you're the only one I know of who was on staff and moved into a leadership position from there. So, talk a little bit about that. In many ways, you know what you're stepping into, don't you?*

Well, it was interesting, because, in talking to Dr. Dobson about it, that was one of the main reasons he liked the idea of me for the job. He said, "You've been around Focus for so long that you've seen all the weaknesses and probably have some ideas on how to improve things." I valued that. I thought that was really interesting on his part. There were probably three outside candidates whom I was made aware of after I became president, and a couple of them were retired generals. So, I was like, *Wow*. That was amazing to be tapped to lead. But in looking back, I think it was wise of Dr. Dobson and the board to select someone from within the organization. Someone who knew the culture and the unspoken requirements of leadership. What was ahead of us to complete the transition would require both soft and hard skills.

I think that Focus would have gone through two or three or maybe even four leaders if they had not picked an inside person, simply because the turmoil of transitions is hard normally and we had a founder who planned on remaining for an undetermined time. That can place a lot of strain on the structure and the people. I've always said that the difficulty with founder transitions is that the very skills God gave them to succeed are not the best skills in transition. Those founder skills, in my observation, are tenacity, which means working through incredible odds to achieve a desired outcome; being detail oriented, which means building into the organization systems to ensure that people are treated correctly and that content is accurate and appropriate; and finally, control, which means nothing is done, even at a very low level, without the founder's approval. In our case, Dr. Dobson started Focus on the Family "in a one-room office with a part-time secretary," as he used to say. So, the founder builds using these skills.

An example of being detail minded was reviewing the wording of the printed materials produced by Focus, which was something Dr. Dobson used to do. I'm talking about hundreds of articles and letters and a large amount of other material every month. That was a lot of responsibility for him because he cared about the brand and the quality of what went out of Focus. So he read almost everything that was created here. He also had a President Reagan–approach to the staff. Trust but verify. To achieve this, he created mechanisms to ensure compliance. The "hot pending" system was an example. He would send a comment or question to any level of staff if he was made aware of a problem. That staff member had twenty-four hours to respond. If she did not respond, he might give her a call to see what the problem was. It could be intimidating. However, these were the systems that worked for him as a founder to control the organization.

Tenacity, detail, and control are good gifts for building an organization, but these gifts can create chaos at transition time. When the transition comes, second-generation leaders tend to be goal driven. They have different gifts. They are not founder driven. Frankly, I don't want to do another person's job. If you are hired to write, then perfect your craft. My job is to run Focus as effectively and efficiently as possible. To achieve that, I am asking, *What are things we can improve on? Is the vision exactly what it needs to be?* And it takes a different skill set to improve something that already exists, as compared with creating it.

*I remember sitting with you a few months ago and hearing some of your thoughts on taking over a team that wasn't yours. What were a couple of key leadership skills that you either learned or brought in with you?*

I think some of them were really difficult. Most of them were fairly easy, such as recognizing the need to cast vision and then reinforce that vision. Those are things that are normal. My leadership style was always relationally oriented, so I struggled to dictate a memo. I really found that a walk-around approach was more suited to me—being with the team, showing up for the morning devotion with them, and talking about where we needed to go, what we needed to do. And for the most part, that worked well for most of the departments at Focus on the Family.

The one area that was most difficult was the public policy area because, I think, this is where there was a distinction between the founder and me. We had different ideas about how to approach the culture. It's partly generational, because Dr. Dobson was a culture warrior like Jerry Falwell and D. James Kennedy. I did a little research, and ironically, all of them were born in the 1930s. I had empathy for this because those who were born in the 1930s, as these gentlemen were, saw a lot of change within the Judeo-Christian value system in the US. So these men, understandably, kind of reacted to what they were losing:

reading the Bible in school, praying in school, and a general consensus within the culture that these principles—the Ten Commandments—were not controversial. There had been this belief of *Yeah, we can't always live up to them, but we generally agree that this is a good social compact, that if we don't murder one another, that's a good thing.* They saw the breakdown of that cohesion and agreement in the culture. So, that gave me a little more understanding of their actions.

But I was born in the 1960s, and I would say I am less prophetic and more evangelistic, and I think those men were very prophetic, saying, "Hey, if we go down this path, we're going to run into trouble as a culture. We need to correct our course when it comes to the definition of marriage, abortion, all those moral issues we as a nation have turned our back on." And there's credence to that. You need prophets declaring what is true and what isn't.

But for me, the question was, How do we reach the culture? How do we influence the culture to understand these moral issues and persuade the culture that the Judeo-Christian approach to these big moral issues is good for the culture?

So, when I walked into the public policy department, I was hearing the whispers: "Jim Daly's no Jim Dobson; he doesn't have a stomach for this. He doesn't agree with the activity in the public policy arena." I knew that this was part of the thinking within this department. This is a group of eighty people within Focus on the Family. I really had to get in there, and I tried to use Scripture like 2 Timothy 2:22–26, which is an insight on how to deal with the world. When you're dealing with the world, deal with them with kindness and gentleness and pray for those who are ensnared by the Enemy so they might come to their senses and escape the snare of the Enemy. That's the paraphrased version of that section of Scripture in 2 Timothy. I started to use that with the team to cast the vision of how we should engage the culture. The question was, How do we achieve that? Do we simply talk about policies, or do we give context for why we're talking about the policies?

That was a big challenge, and over time, I think those people who didn't deem me worthy of their allegiance left. And that was okay in the end.

*That's a perfect example, too, because there was something you knew needed to be changed. Talk to me about the patience required. How did you stay patient, and what did that look like practically—a boots-on-the-ground kind of thing?*

It was difficult for those five years from 2005 to 2010 when I was president but couldn't really make independent decisions. The first three years went very well. The last two years had a little more bruising, as I had to make more difficult decisions around budget and emphasis. I also had to know with conviction what the Lord was calling me to do. What was it He expected of my leadership? And was it consistent with Scripture? I felt kind of caught, trying to manage the pace at which I could do these things with Dr. Dobson still involved. It felt at times like I was in second gear. But then I had a younger management team that I put in place who wanted more aggressive change. That was a tremendous challenge. I wanted to honor the founder but hang on to these talented young leaders. I had to let some of those leaders go because the tension was too great.

I went through a top-level management team over the course of five years. Most of that top-level team burned out at some point and just felt it wasn't moving fast enough. But, again, I had to stay true to making sure there was as much peace in that transition as I could provide in my leadership role. And I think the Lord honored that.

The next wave of my C-team has been solid. And we've been intact now for ten years. It's been terrific. What you mentioned is really critical. Sometimes the key leadership requirement is to go not so fast that you outrun the founder nor so slow that you're not moving with the Lord. And that's an art. It's a feel for the organization, the people, and the mission.

*It's a dance. I mean, it really is. In the first section of this book, I talked about the importance of the fruit of the Spirit. If you're in a position like this and you exhibit the fruit of the Spirit, that's a pretty good start.*

Absolutely. I think that's pitch perfect. I used that a lot in my walk-arounds at Focus during the transition. The fruit of the Spirit. I used to go to Galatians 5:19–21 and say, "Well, let's look at the other fruit, which is dissension, strife, envy, sowing seeds of discord—that's the fruit of the other guy. It gets pretty close to the heart. And right at this moment in Focus's history—in the transition—we all have to watch being rooted in the wrong fruit."

That became very helpful for me. And I called out a lot of people, including myself at times. "Let's back up. Let's get rooted in God's fruit and behave in a way that's worthy of the calling of Christ." And I'm serious. I mean, that was a constant daily battle for me—both to require it and to live it.

*Because it's hard! Let's talk about your devotional life during that time. Why did it matter to you that you stayed consistent in prayer and reading the Word?*

It was really the only thing that was stable. I mean, the thing is, people of goodwill can have a lot of different ideas about how we engage the culture and how we execute ministry and how we do these things in a way that honors God. And if you're not rooted in the Word and if you're not hearing the Holy Spirit speaking to your heart first and foremost, then you're going to make errors. If we were all more aware of this, I think we'd have an entirely different church. If we were quick to think of our own shortcomings before going after the other guy's shortcomings with no empathy. It doesn't mean the other person's positions aren't wrong. It just means that having a less pointed attitude gives us a little more humility and empathy as we speak to others. It makes us better people when we're more humble in that way.

Another issue was that I was not sleeping well with all the stress. We decided that we would make the transition at the same time that we ended up having the economic downturn, the real estate bubble of 2007 to 2008. We later joked that it must have been God's divine plan. We had rapidly declining revenue. Dr. Dobson was still at Focus, but we had lost about $10 to 15 million in revenue. So I had to make adjustments. At the same time, I was being criticized by Dr. Dobson while I was trying to keep the organization afloat. That was really hard for me emotionally, and I was getting one or two hours of sleep a night for about a year and a half. During about a three-year period, I had to lay off about six hundred staff, and that was hard for me. It never became easy. The lesson learned was to allow God to carry that yoke. It was too heavy.

These were big decisions. I mean, if I had not made those decisions, we would have been out of business, out of ministry, if you can think of that. We cut $15 million, and we ended the next year $100,000 in the black, and we had no line of credit. We lived off a principle that we would spend everything that came in and would keep a six-week reserve.

Now, think of managing in that environment. I mean, it was hard and I wasn't sleeping. I've really felt, though, that being an orphan kid was a big help in that circumstance. The Lord does equip you for the moment He calls you to. There were so many dynamics about my childhood that came into play with the transition, in terms of trusting the Lord and being faithful even when circumstances aren't favorable. It was a good opportunity for me to help other people around me be more confident in Christ. I think we all grew in that context and even now are growing.

In 2011 and 2012, I finally felt like we were getting oxygen again. We came up for air, we had our first positive budget, and it was really good! And it's been that way ever since.

So, yeah, being in the Word, being in prayer . . . it's when you're in those circumstances that you grow and better understand who you are. I've realized that you learn very little on the mountaintop. You learn most of your core lessons about your own character and God's character in the valley. The blessings can blind you if you're not careful. And God knows that.

*So, you'd been there, and you knew there were some cultural things inside that needed to change. There were some cultural realities that you wanted to make progress on. How did you get the team to buy into a new culture, into a new way of doing things?*

I think on the one hand there was a lot of excitement about what Focus was doing. Generally, you could walk into the office every day with a little skip in your step because it's great to save marriages, save babies' lives with our ultrasound programs, and do the other things we were doing. With the daily broadcast, of course, we'd get immediate feedback from the people whose lives we'd touched. As an example, my wife's brother committed suicide years ago. I had Jean on to talk about the pain of that and the guilt she experienced as a family member. Probably about three thirty in the afternoon the day that broadcast aired, we got a phone call here at Focus from a woman who was going to take her life but heard Jean's story. And because of what Jean said, it kept the woman from taking her life.

I remember getting home that night and telling Jean—it chokes me up now talking about it—"Man, you saved someone's life today because of what you suffered through." And we get to experience that almost every day here—that kind of kingdom magic that occurs when a marriage is saved or a woman decides to keep a baby that she was going to abort. So, that's extremely rewarding.

The core stuff was here, and for me, it was just reemphasizing God's heart for people and that His grace is sufficient. I think we, through Dr. Dobson's leadership, drifted into a course where winning in the political arena or winning in a contest of ideas became more critical. That may be unfair, but that was my perspective. I was forming the idea that it's not about winning; it's about being faithful to Christ, and that, ultimately, is what we have to do. Was Peter congratulated for chopping off the servant's ear in the garden? No, he was rebuked by Christ. However, Stephen, who was stoned to death, prayed for those persecuting him and asked the Lord to forgive them. I contend that a person can do that only by being filled with the Spirit of God. If we are in the flesh, we will exhibit bad fruit.

Back to the fruit of the Spirit example that you gave. If you are all about winning the contest rather than being faithful in the contest, you've lost, because in that arena you will pull out tools from your human toolbox that are antithetical to the fruit of the Spirit. I went to lunch with David Horowitz, the former communist from Berkeley who's written a book called *Dark Agenda: The War to Destroy Christian America,* which is about how the left is deconstructing Christianity in America. We were at lunch, and he's not a Christian. And he said to me, "Jim, don't you know you're in an alley fight and the other side has switch-blades? You've got to come to fight!" And I said, "David, the problem is we're not allowed to bring a switchblade. We must bring the fruit of the Spirit to the fight, which is what Jesus did. He didn't go into those fights with hordes of militants. He went in with people who were loving and kind and good and willing to lay their lives down for those accusing them. It's a completely different way that this warfare is fought."

I remember he sat back at lunch and said, "I never realized that."

To me, that's the core issue. And that's really the difference between Peter in the garden strapping on his weapon to go to battle and the Lord rebuking him and saying, "That's not My kingdom. That's not how My kingdom functions." He healed the servant. And you know what? Who thinks Peter was going after the dude's ear? He was going for his throat, man!

Then there's Stephen, filled with the Holy Spirit. In Peter's defense, in his case, the Lord had not been crucified and resurrected, and the Holy Spirit hadn't been given to all of us. But in Stephen's case, the Holy Spirit had been given. Post-Resurrection, Stephen could be filled with the Holy Spirit, so he could pray for those who were killing him. Scripture says that the heavens opened up and Stephen saw Jesus standing at the right hand of God. So, Stephen got a standing ovation from Jesus, and Peter got the rebuke. And that's always been a good guide for me in the cultural battle. Am I acting more like Peter, which is what my flesh wants to do? Or am I acting more like Stephen, which is what God's Spirit wants me to do? And that's tough.

*It's tough, but it's real. And that's because we're human. When you came in, what was your biggest fear stepping into that space?*

I think I didn't fear failure because I'm already a failure! I didn't come from this great family. I'm an orphan kid. I just didn't have that fear of "I can't measure up." I did have a fear that I could mess it up. I've always felt like I'll just do the best I can do. And God has given me that resil-iency to say to myself, "If you're doing your best, God will honor it." I had a fear that I wasn't equipped adequately, because who am I to lead a group like Focus? Unlike Dr. Dobson, who has a PhD in child development, had spent countless hours counseling married couples, and had spent time at the USC School of Medicine. His professional credentials were pretty good. As for me, I just had to live the hard knocks of life!

One of my observations that was really funny was thinking about all the family types I had lived in—the typical dysfunctional mom and dad, then my single-parent mom. I lived with a foster family after my mom died. I had a stepfather. I ended up living with my single-parent dad for a year. Then he passed away. I lived with my brother throughout high school. The only family structure I didn't experience as a child was living with my grandparents, because I didn't have grandparents.

The night before I was made president of Focus, I was wrestling with all this and my inadequacy in terms of my training. And I remember the Lord saying, *I own it all. I own what was good, including Dr. Dobson coming from a stable family, and I own what you had to come from. It's all Mine. Just be yielded to Me.* It was in the middle of the night when He spoke that into my heart. I just remember settling down and saying, *Okay.* I felt God saying, *Listen. I allowed you to live in just about every family type you could live in so you'll know the experiences of those people who are going to write and call asking for help. It's not the clinical experience that you've gained, but it's the real-life experience that you gained.* And I think that's really close to God's heart. That's good. Because that's what brokenness is. I mean, you can know it intellectually, but if you've had to live it, it's a lot different. When your tears are falling on the pillow as an eight-year-old boy or girl, it makes loneliness very real.

*What would your advice be if you were sitting with a couple of new leaders who were stepping into new places to lead things they didn't start? What are one or two things you would say to encourage them?*

I think one thing for me would be the patience aspect of it. One of the things I've seen in the twenty- to thirtysomethings who are working at Focus is that they really want to see themselves rise to the VP level or the executive level very quickly. And again, in my experience, time is a good thing. It's like marriage. I was talking to a gentleman yesterday, a donor for Focus who lives in Oklahoma, and he was talking about his marriage and where it's at right now. He said, "The first fifteen to twenty years, it's chaos because you're raising kids. And you're learning about each other, knowing each other, loving each other. It's just kind of settling in. And then in that middle section, you're climbing. You're accomplishing those goals that you had, but you're disconnected. Now that I'm fifty-five years old and moving into that last third," he said, "the comfort level that I'm experiencing in my marriage right now is amazing. It's like we know each other. We are comfortable in a good way with each other, and it's just good to be with each other."

I thought, *That is so true.* And I think it's real on the employment side too. Be patient, and work as hard as you can. Do the best job you can do in the role God's given you in that moment. And then trust that the right people will notice that you're doing well and that you can take on more responsibility. That's what I did. That's how it worked for me at Focus. I don't want to underemphasize being faithful to the task at hand. Don't have your eye on the next thing, which means you do the current thing in a mediocre way. Do really well what God has in front of you. Then He'll open up to you the next thing.

Second, be prepared. That's the best advice I received—finish my MBA, and do those things that make me capable and give me the skill set to operate in a proficient way with the things God has given me. For King David, it was slinging that stone as he was out there in the field. Man, he was good at it! He got good at it because, as Malcolm Gladwell wrote in *David and Goliath,* he probably did it over ten thousand hours. Ten thousand hours of slinging a stone, and he became proficient at it. And that's the same thing for us. No one saw David slinging those stones, but God saw David and knew he could do the job.

That's the concern I have with the younger folks: have the patience to practice your skill set until you're really proficient at it, whatever it might be. Managing people, casting vision, accomplishing tasks—whatever. Then allow God to direct your path.

# 16

=

## JIMMY ROLLINS:
### *Lead Pastor of i5 City*

IT WOULDN'T WORK FOR ME TO TALK TO AMAZING LEADERS WITHOUT HEAR-
ing from a pastor! As I mentioned earlier, I believe in the next couple of
decades, we will see many founding pastors having to hand off their
churches to others. My twenty-plus years in ministry keep my heart
and attention on how to help us make this transition well.

Pastor Jimmy Rollins will be the first to admit that he didn't lead the
transition perfectly. But when you inherit the church your parents
started . . . it's never going to be easy. Jimmy is one of the most humble, kind, and strategic leaders I know. It's been an honor to learn from
him, and I'm excited for you to learn from him as well.

*Here's a little about Jimmy's story in his own words.*

I started by working with my parents in the church they founded in
1994—an amazing outreach-centered church. They were part of a de-
nomination and wanted to do something locally in their own community. We were traveling about forty minutes down to Washington, DC,
to do street ministry, but they wanted to start something in our own
area. So, in 1994, they planted, or launched, a church—back then the
word wasn't *planted;* you just started a church.

It was called Living Waters Worship Center, and God blessed it.
God's hand was on it, and I think it grew over the years to about seven
hundred people. And here's the deal: God was moving, and it was
great. Church on Sunday was great, but I just had these ideas that the
church could be diverse. If the gospel message is as great as we say it

is on Sundays, why is it not infiltrating Monday, Tuesday, Wednesday, Thursday, Friday, and Saturday?

So I started just kind of bumping up against what we were doing.

In 2011, we started having conversations of transfer, of succession, of who's next and what we're going to do. And we thought it was going to be amazing until my mom and dad found out that I really wanted to do something different—we had hard conversations, like changing the name of the church and going after a diverse group of people. We were primarily African American. Hard conversations about providing more ministry outside the four walls of the church.

Honestly, I wouldn't trade one second of the lessons that were learned during that season and the wisdom that was gained and the failures that were experienced—they really made me the leader I am today.

*Let's talk about a couple of those. What one or two things did you learn early on that you knew, If I don't do this, I don't know if we're going to make it?*

I think one of the things is putting the *why* behind the *what*. Whenever we're discussing change or we're implementing change, we have to bring people along the journey of that. My idea was not a good idea; it was a God idea; but I needed to bring people along the journey by giving them the *why*. What's behind the *what*? Why were we going to change the name? Why were we not going to be a church that was title driven? Why were we looking for a diverse group of people? Not even just ethnically diverse but socioeconomically, gender-wise, and generationally.

So, one of the main things that I did not do well in the beginning was giving the *why* behind the *what*. And if I had to go back and talk to myself in 2011, I'd say, "Hey, Jimmy, take people along the journey. People have invested their time, their energy, their resources into this church. You need to understand that. You need to give them time to catch up with the vision that God has for this church." So, the *why* behind the *what* would probably be the number one thing that I wish I had done better.

*It's tricky, isn't it? You can't come in guns blazing like a new sheriff in town without a why. Yes, you may have the right to do that, but it's not a win, is it?*

No, it wasn't a win. And, honestly, at forty-six years old now, I know that back then I was just young and dumb and thought that my ideas were the best ideas. And the second thing I would say is that new is not better. That new is just different. And I think a lot of times we think that we have the best ideas. We think that our environment is going to be better because of lights and haze. And we really don't embrace legacy, and we think that new is better, not just different.

One of the things that I have really leaned into with my guys is this: "Your ideas are great, but you need to build on the foundation of what was established before you."

Now, one of the things that I like to say is that every transition begins with an ending and ends with a new beginning. I'll say that again: every transition begins with an ending and ends with a new beginning.

What I really wanted to do was the best. And I'll never forget—I had a conversation with my daughter, and she said, "Dad, I think how you're handling this needs to be different." And she continued, "Because one day I'm going to hate your ideas." She was telling me to look at it differently because the generation behind might not like the direction. So, try to think about the next generation who might come after you.

*Wow.*

And that kind of settled in with me, Tyler. That's strong, right?

*I can imagine. I'm sitting here thinking about my son saying that too. I was like, Wow. The next question would be, "Now what?" How did you evaluate where you felt like you needed to go?*

Well, I think what I didn't do well was evaluate. Ideas are great, but ideas without metrics, right? Like what you measure matters. And we weren't measuring anything. They were just great ideas that had no statistics, no measurements. Back then they were just, "Hey, I think this is going to be cooler. I think we're going to attract more people." But what we didn't realize is that younger people . . . you can attract all you want. But there's something about legacy. Younger people don't have wisdom. Younger people don't have discernment. Younger people can't be mentors. So, I wish I had bridged the gap through evaluating. What were the needs of the people coming in the building—the newer people, the younger people who we were attracting? Their main needs were wisdom and mentorship, but I had ticked off all the older people, so I had nobody to mentor the new, younger people!

We grew fast, but it wasn't healthy growth. We were an immature church. And when you're immature and life hits you and you have no one to talk to or talk through it with, now you're going to start projecting those things onto other people. And now it's the church's fault—"You weren't there for me." But we didn't have anything structurally set up to minister to the people who we were actually going after.

So, I wish I had met with every person who had been a part of my mom and dad's church and asked, "What do you want to see in church?" And I wish I had bridged the gap of talking to them about their grandchildren and everything. Telling them that I was called to make sure that their spiritual inheritance and their spiritual legacy were insured for their children and their children's children. I could have brought them along the journey.

One of the greatest evaluations is not even something that we could have put in a computer or we could have put on a spreadsheet. It's the evaluation of how your heart is connected to the next generation.

*You've got to have a gauge on that, don't you? You have to understand it so that you can then make some plans accordingly. One of the things I talked about earlier in the book is the fruit of the Spirit. When we go into these places, if we start with the fruit of the Spirit, that's a pretty good starting spot. But the one issue that I really spend some time on is patience, because when you take over and you transition, patience is massively important. Can you talk a little bit about how patience has played a role for you in this transition?*

Tyler, I'm just going to be completely up front. Like a lot of people look at what we're doing now and say, "Man, it's amazing. What you guys are doing at i5 Church is great."

I had no patience. Honestly, we would probably be double the number we are today. Our impact would be greater and our influence would be broader if I'd had patience. I have a lot of regrets. I have a lot of regrets about how we transitioned, because I didn't have much patience. I thought that everything had to happen now. I thought that everything had to happen immediately. I thought that waiting was dumb, and when people were saying, "Let me get back to you," I took that as offense. That's because I was an insecure young leader who thought he knew everything. And it's easy now for me to spot guys who just need to slow down.

*So, what happened that made you realize that?*

Self-inflicted wounds!

*Can you remember a specific time or example of this?*

I can just remember a time with some people who God had sent to my mom and dad's church to ensure the legacy of the church. But because I didn't have patience and allow them to embrace and go through the process, we lost great people. And now as a leader, I see that some of these people still haven't landed. And they haven't landed eight years later because they were supposed to be with us.

But my lack of patience and my insecurities really got us to a place where our foundation could have been a lot stronger. So, going through that process of learning how to give the *why* behind the *what,* I wish I had understood.

I read a book called *Who Stole My Church?* and understood generationally how people saw church. It's different from how we see church now. Back in my mom and dad's day, there wasn't a lot of church hopping, because people looked at their church as more than just their place to meet God. It was community. It was family. It was legacy. It was a pillar in the community. And I didn't really understand that, given that at the time I was thirty-six or thirty-seven years old.

Now let's talk about long runways, right? Let's talk about strategic planning. I didn't know what a strategic plan was. A strategic plan was what God told me in the bathroom the night before that I had to do the next day.

*And that's not always the best strategic plan, is it? You obviously inherited some people. I'm assuming you had some team members that just didn't seem to be getting on board with you and the new direction, some players who were saying, "I don't know if I'm with you." How did you lead them? What's something you learned as a way to manage that?*

Well, I think it's all core values. So, for us, we've got three core values that govern everything we do: live beyond yourself, love beyond your preferences, and laugh beyond your struggles.

We don't want to be selfish. We want to be selfless. Are the decisions that we're making others generated? Are they others focused? We want to love beyond our preferences, which means my ideas are not going to be the best ideas. And can I embrace something that's not my particular preference for the cause of the organization?

The last one would be laugh beyond your struggles. Are we having fun? Is this going to cause us to have more fun?

So, what happens is . . . if we hire based off those values, then when an idea comes to the table that's not our taste and not our preference, is it going to be selfless and is it going to be fun? If we put everything up against those three values, then I can have staff that disagrees with me or a team that disagrees with me or I can disagree with them and still implement it.

And we have to go through those things. I wish I'd had these core values from day one—a decision matrix based off those things. I wish I'd understood that my preference is not going to grow our church but God's presence will, and sometimes it comes in a way that I don't necessarily see or understand.

*One of the things I've admired about you from a distance is that I feel you're a culture builder. Talk about the value of culture creation as you're moving into an inherited space.*

Well, I think it's key. When we're looking at culture, we have to understand that first of all we want a life-giving culture. If it's a life-giving culture, healthy things grow. If something's not growing, it's probably a product not of people's performance but of the culture that they're performing in.

Culture is key when you're changing—when you've been a church that's typically inward and you want to go outward or you're an organization that is doing business in this area and you want to go to this other area. First of all, before you change anything, have you built a culture of change? Because what I wish I knew back then is there's something called change fatigue. Without a culture of change, people become change fatigued because they're just not used to change. Right?

I'll tell you this—one of the things I wish I had done was build a culture of "We're going to try this" rather than "This is going to be the best thing ever!" Or "This sermon is going to be the best!" Or "This weekend will be amazing!" We had a big announcement every week! I see all these guys doing that, and I'm like, "That's not a culture of change. Right? That's not a culture of the *why* behind the *what*."

I should have built a culture of "We're going to try this." I should have underpromised and overdelivered. Instead of overpromising and underdelivering what I said was supposed to be so amazing. It actually wasn't amazing, because we didn't study the metrics. We didn't have a culture of change.

I should have built a culture of change, and then I would've built a culture of "taking the L," and I'll explain that. Taking the L (or taking the loss) is as a leader being okay to say what you're not. Being okay to say where you blew it. Being okay to say, "I thought this was going to be a great idea, and it didn't work out." And owning the gap.

And I wish I had done that. And now, honestly, I try as much as possible. Back then I very rarely dropped the "God said," but I had come out of that culture—that's what you said when you wanted to do something: "This is what the Lord has spoken to me." No, that was gas!

*You've been very candid, and I appreciate your honesty. What was a fear of yours when you stepped in? Like first day, first week, first month? What fear in your heart and in your spirit did you have to wrestle with?*

I had to wrestle with the fear of losing my immediate family. That was probably the biggest thing because, honestly, that season wasn't great. I'll call it "brutaful"—kind of beautiful and brutal all at the same time. I had a high fear of just not being in relationship with my family, and to be honest with you, that was our case for three or four years.

The pain of changing. The pain of changing without my mom and dad necessarily embracing what we were doing. The pain of—which was probably 70 percent my fault—rejection from people you did life with. I think I feared rejection. I think I feared failure. Like as far as, *What if this doesn't work? What if we spent all this money, all these resources, all this time on something that was just a good idea, not a God idea?*

I feared failure. And I'm going to tell you why. The biggest thing that I think I could say to leaders who are thinking about succession is to ask yourself the question, "Why? What's my win?" And I think my win was not more impact and more influence. I think my win was, "Let me feel good about myself."

Let me give leaders a caution. I'll say it this way: Is winning at the wrong thing worth it? So, in succession, is it about impact? Is it about people? Is it about influence for God and the kingdom of God rather than you building a big church? What's going on inside you?

We live in this culture of Instagram and Facebook and Twitter where we're saying, "Hey, look what I can accomplish, and look what I can do." That is driving us rather than being an influence for the gospel message of Jesus Christ.

Honestly, when you're young, you want more followers, you want more likes. But I've learned how to play for an audience of one. And I've learned that if I'm trying to please people, I'm probably not pleasing God.

Pain is the greatest teacher anybody could ever have.

I didn't always think like I think now. I didn't always respond like I respond now. I didn't always take time for the things that I take time for now. And I feared losing my family. And I did. This transition of leadership was filled with good and bad decisions, so our family relationships were hurt.

And it's taken years to get back. And I thank God that He's a healer. I thank God that He's a redeemer and He's a fixer. And He's done that, but there was a lot of time that I was building a church and not building a family.

*I worked with Andy Stanley for a decade, and one of the things he used to always say was, "We're not called to sacrifice our families on the altar of ministry." And that's a real thing.*

*If you were going to lunch today with a twenty-five-year-old guy or girl who's about to step into a team that already exists, what's the one piece of advice that you would leave him or her with and say, "As you go in today, think about this"?*

Honor. You cannot go wrong with honor. Honor who was there before you; honor the customers or the people or the congregation who was there before you. Keep yourself low. Come in as a learner; be a lifetime learner. An idea without wisdom is stupidity.

Tyler, I love these opportunities because people don't really know me. Like they see me traveling and preaching, and I get it. And they think that's a big deal. And I promise you, man, for me it's not. I can't believe that God still uses me. I was young and stupid.

I can't believe what God's doing. I find myself more now, when I go to preach, looking forward to talking to the pastors and the people about our story. I was just at Southeastern University, and I stayed over to hang with young people. I don't want to be whisked away and go back to the green room. I want to pray for kids. I want to be fully present in the environment that I'm in. I want to help the local pastor build his church. I want to help. I feel more like the old-school word for me would be *apostolic* rather than *evangelistic.*

I think we're in trouble, if I'm honest with you. I think we're still "celebritizing"—that's not going to work. We're putting celebrities on a platform instead of putting the gospel on a platform.

*Well, I think guys like you who are fighting for the right things are helping with that. And, honestly, my whole career has been leadership based because I believe that how we lead affects people's faith almost more than anything. So, as someone who's a newer friend to you but someone who's grateful for how you lead, I just want to say thanks for taking the time but also thanks for the way you're leading.*

Oh, man, I'm trying. I'm just trying to steward my piece, man. Be a good steward of what God's given me. It's different at forty-six than it was at thirty-six.

# 17

## A Charge

I'VE THOUGHT LONG AND HARD ABOUT WHAT I WANT TO LEAVE YOU WITH. What charge can I send you off with to help you succeed as you step into or continue leading something you didn't start?

The answer became quite obvious to me.

It's twofold. First, a simple reminder of the process:

**E**valuation
**P**atience
**I**mplementation
**C**are

If you noticed, care wasn't a section all by itself. Everything we talked about was people focused, and that's why *care* lives everywhere in the process. It has to be the paper you write your values on. It needs to be the fabric of the culture and implementation. If you care for people well, you will see success as you inherit another team. But care comes from a place of character.

The second thought goes back to where we started. I know it will take you further than your skill or talent can ever take you. Further than your network or pedigree. Further than all of that combined.

> The fruit of the Spirit is love, joy, peace, patience, kindness, goodness, faithfulness, gentleness, self-control; against such things there is no law. . . .
>
> If we live by the Spirit, let us also keep in step with the Spirit.[1]

Leader, this is the best next step. This is the best daily step.
First, look up so you can stay in step with the Spirit.
Second, watch the fruit change those around you forever.
Lead well and give life.

# Thirty-Day EPIC Plan

As WE PREPARE TO WALK INTO A TEAM, ORGANIZATION, OR OTHER SPACE that we inherit, we need to have a simple plan. A map to keep our eyes on the prize. *Focus.*

Remember this:

**E***valuation*
**P***atience*
**I***mplementation*
**C***are*

Breaking the challenge down by day can be a little too limiting, so I'm suggesting you make some decisions for each week. There isn't a perfect formula. There's just direction.

As you think about each week you're stepping into, remember the fruit of the Spirit. All four phases need gentleness, love, joy, and so on. Keep that in mind. So, each week you will take the big ideas and decide what days you'll do what.

Let me say this: *It's not going to be perfect.* You're working with imperfect people. You're imperfect. But that's okay. This plan will work for the people you're now influencing, and this plan will work for you as well. You will have to keep evaluation of *yourself* front and center to recalibrate when needed. You will need to be patient with *yourself,* which is harder than most of the other parts of the plan. You will then be ready to start implementing new culture, vision, and direction.

At the end of the day, you have to cover with *care* this entire process and the people you are leading. Put all these plans on the paper of care. Care for yourself and care for the team around you.

With this in mind, here's a simple road map to get you started.[1]

# Week One

1. Pray. Before you even walk in the building, pray.
   + Pray for those you're inheriting. By name.
   + Pray for wisdom and discernment.
   + Pray for the fruit of the Spirit.
   + Pray for yourself.
   + Pray for patience.

2. Evaluation. During week one, you need some "big rock" understanding. In other words, what are the biggest areas you need to get a grasp on?
   + Financial realities (not deep dive, just big picture)
   + Team realities

     *You have to start creating a safe place from day one.*

     *Make it clear you are safe through conversations.*
   + Processes

     *Are there any?*

     *What's missing according to the team?*

     *What's the external reputation of the organization or team?*
   + Wins

     *What small wins does the team need in order to wake up? In other words, think through a couple of achievable goals that show the team they can be successful with this new direction.*

+ Fires
  *Are there any immediate fires to extinguish?*

3. Patience
   + Think through one or two areas you know you'll have to be patient with during week one so you're prepared to take your time.

4. Implementation
   + Not yet. Unless there is a glaring issue that has to be immediately addressed.

5. Care
   + Get to know the team.
   + Ask them questions about their lives.
   + Enjoy some meals together.

# Week Two

1. Pray
   + Pray for those you're inheriting. By name.
   + Pray for wisdom and discernment.
   + Pray for the fruit of the Spirit.
   + Pray for yourself.
   + Pray for patience.

2. Evaluation
   + Time to get a little more micro based on what you learned last week.
   + Where are the financials? What needs to be understood better?
   + Cultural questionnaire: Develop a survey for the current culture and where it's winning and losing. Ask questions about the state of the current culture.
   + Organizational structure: Is it right? Does it make sense?
   + How's the overall team environment and mojo right now?

3. Patience
   + Unless something's on fire, just wait.

4. Implementation
   + Is there anything from last week that needs to be course corrected immediately?
   + Are there one or two small cultural adjustments you want to make for positive movement?
   + What are one or two things you can start sharing about vision? The future?

5. Care
   + Get to know the names of the spouses of your team members. This is a simple but strong step toward care.

# Week Three

1. Pray
   + Pray for those you're inheriting. By name.
   + Pray for wisdom and discernment.
   + Pray for the fruit of the Spirit.
   + Pray for yourself.
   + Pray for patience.

2. Evaluation
   + After two weeks, what continues to need attention?
   + What does the team obviously not want to change?
   + What land mines are waiting to be stepped on?
   + What's missing to make the team successful?
   + Who on the team is going to move well into this transition, and who needs coaching?
   + What needs immediate change?
   + What can wait?

3. Patience
   + Where are you dying to make a change but know you have to be patient?
   + Where has past leadership moved too fast? In other words, where did the last leaders not count the costs of decisions and actually hurt

the business and team rather than helping them?

4. Implementation
   + What should your next cultural adjustments be?
   + Have a team fun time. Just hang out with no agenda.
   + Make sure one-on-ones are happening with key leaders.
   + What can you do this week to model one or two new leadership directions?

5. Care
   + Don't forget to *care*!

# Week Four

1. Pray
   + Pray for those you're inheriting. By name.
   + Pray for wisdom and discernment.
   + Pray for the fruit of the Spirit.
   + Pray for yourself.
   + Pray for patience.

2. Evaluation
   + What's working during this first month?
   + Which areas of change are getting traction, and which ones aren't?
   + Where have fears shown up—either in you or in the team—and how can you address them?
   + How's the team doing?
   + How's your understanding of the overall financial model and what needs changing?
   + Who has stepped up with proper motives?

3. Patience
   + Write down two or three team members you know you're going to need to be extra patient with, as well as how long you'd like to give each person to make adjustments. This is your game plan, so make sure your emotions don't get the best of you.

4. Implementation
   + Focus this week on moving the ball down the
     field in the following areas:
     *Culture*
     *Vision*
     *Leading the way*

5. Care
   + Take five minutes each day to check in on the
     lives of those you lead.

# Acknowledgments

I NEVER THOUGHT I'D WRITE ONE BOOK. TWO? YOU'RE CRAZY. WHAT AN honor. I'm praying that this book will help many leaders lead to their fullest potential when they step into some interesting spots.

You can't write one book, much less two, without a small army of people in your corner. I've always been unbelievably grateful to those who decide to stand with me no matter what!

Thank you to my wife, Carrie. We are coming up on twenty years of marriage, and I couldn't imagine a better life partner. You've pushed me to do more than I ever thought possible. Let's do this another twenty!

To my two boys, Nate and Charlie. Other than your mom, you two take the cake. I can't believe how you're growing up into amazing young men. You are teaching me how to display the fruit of the Spirit, because I see it in you!

I want to say a quick thanks to the leaders who've worked on this project with me. Thanks to my agents, Curtis Yates and Mike Salisbury, for fighting for this book and helping me get it across the finish line. I know I'm not your biggest-selling client, but I wouldn't know that by how you treat me and fight for me.

Thank you to Bruce Nygren for walking with me word by word to get this bad boy edited and corrected.

A huge thank-you to the entire team at WaterBrook. I couldn't be prouder to be one of your authors. Andrew Stoddard, you're a legend and great friend. Thanks for leading this project as always!

Thank you to Coach Buzz Williams, Cheryl Bachelder, Jim Daly, and

Pastor Jimmy Rollins for sharing your stories of inherited leadership so other leaders can learn from you.

Thanks, Cara Shroyer, for coming out of retirement to keep me in order for the second time in your career!

Lastly, thanks to all the leaders I've watched lead and bring life to those they lead. Especially when they've inherited something.

# Notes

## Chapter 1: Inheriting Influence

1. Galatians 5:22–23.

## Chapter 2: Good Fruit

1. Ty Kiisel, "65% of Americans Choose a Better Boss over a Raise—Here's Why," *Forbes,* October 16, 2012, www.forbes.com/sites/tykiisel/2012/10/16/65-of-americans-choose-a-better-boss-over-a-raise-heres-why/#7235de3976d2.
2. Matthew 7:14.
3. Romans 8:9–14, MSG.

## Chapter 3: The New Kid on the Block

The epigraph is taken from " 'You've Got to Find What You Love,' Jobs Says," Stanford News, June 14, 2005, https://news.stanford.edu/2005/06/14/jobs-061505.

## Section 2: The Importance of Honoring and Learning from the Past

1. Psalm 121:1.

## CHAPTER 4: HONORING THE PAST WITHOUT GETTING TRAPPED BY IT

The epigraph is taken from Jacqueline Novogratz, "Inspiring a Life of Immersion," TEDWomen 2010, December 2010, 17:31, www.ted.com/talks/jacqueline _novogratz_inspiring_a_life_of_immersion /transcript?language=en.

1. For more information, visit onsiteworkshops.com.
2. Steven Pressfield, *The War of Art: Break Through the Blocks and Win Your Inner Creative Battles* (New York: Black Irish Entertainment, 2002), 90.
3. *The Hunger Games,* directed by Gary Ross (Santa Monica, CA: Lionsgate, 2012).
4. Andy Stanley, North Point Community Church staff meeting, Alpharetta, GA.
5. Simon Sinek, "Start with Why: How Great Leaders Inspire Action," TEDx, September 28, 2009, 18:01, https://m .youtube.com/watch?vl=en&v=u4ZoJKF_VuA.
6. Matthew 13:52, TPT, emphasis added.

## CHAPTER 5: FRESH EYES

The epigraph is taken from a sermon by Steven Furtick, Elevation Church, October 2015.

## CHAPTER 6: EVALUATION IS BRUTAL BUT NECESSARY

The epigraph is taken from John Wooden and Steve Jamison, *Wooden: A Lifetime of Observations and Reflections on and off the Court* (New York: McGraw-Hill, 1997), 56.

1. Steven Pressfield, *The War of Art: Break Through the Blocks and Win Your Inner Creative Battles* (New York: Black Irish Entertainment, 2002), 88.

## Section 3: Patience Dictates the Success of Inheritance: Three Keys to Waiting

1. Hillsong Worship, "Seasons," by Chris Davenport, Benjamin Hastings, and Ben Tan, *The Peace Project,* Hillsong Church, 2017.

## Chapter 8: Trust the Process: Seeds Don't Grow Overnight

The epigraph is taken from Rudyard Kipling, "The Glory of the Garden," in *Selected Poems,* ed. Peter Keating (London: Penguin Books, 2000), 148.

1. Walter Mischel, Ebbe B. Ebbesen, and Antonette Raskoff Zeiss, "Cognitive and Attentional Mechanisms in Delay of Gratification," *Journal of Personality and Social Psychology* 21, no. 2 (1972): 204–18, https://higher-order-thinking.com /wp-content/uploads/2018/09/cognitive_and_attentional _mechanisms_in_delay_of_gratification.pdf.

2. James Clear, "40 Years of Stanford Research Found That People with This One Quality Are More Likely to Succeed," James Clear, https://jamesclear.com/delayed-gratification.

3. Clear, "40 Years of Stanford Research."

4. Romans 8:28.

5. Hillsong Worship, "Seasons," by Chris Davenport, Benjamin Hastings, and Ben Tan, *The Peace Project,* Hillsong Church, 2017.

6. Danny Lewis, "Death Valley Bursts to Life with Rare 'Super Bloom,'" *Smithsonian,* February 23, 2016, www .smithsonianmag.com/smart-news/death-valley-bursts -life-rare-super-bloom-180958194.

7. Wikipedia, s.v. "Superbloom," https://en.m.wikipedia.org /wiki/Superbloom.

8. Harold Bloom, ed., *Franz Kafka* (Langhorne, PA: Chelsea House, 2005), 62.

9. Matthew 25:24–27.

## CHAPTER 9: INSTANT ISN'T SUSTAINABLE: IF GOD'S NOT DONE WORKING, I'M NOT DONE WAITING

The epigraph is taken from Ray Kroc and Robert Anderson, *Grinding It Out: The Making of McDonald's* (New York: St. Martin's Paperbacks, 1987), 101.

1. Hillsong Worship, "Seasons," by Chris Davenport, Benjamin Hastings, and Ben Tan, *The Peace Project*, Hillsong Church, 2017.

## CHAPTER 10: THE CULTURE GAME

The epigraph is taken from Simon Sinek, Facebook, August 12, 2018, www.facebook.com/simonsinek /posts/10156599835606499.

1. Patrick Lencioni, *The Five Dysfunctions of a Team: A Leadership Fable* (San Francisco: Jossey-Bass, 2002).

## CHAPTER 12: 4D MODELING

The epigraph is taken from Michael Hyatt, interview by Jim Bradford, "Inside the C-Suite: Mike Hyatt," Vanderbilt Owen Graduate School of Management, January 17, 2011, YouTube video, 24:34, www.youtube .com/watch?v=w8ryfmoDUcU.

1. Benjamin Franklin, *Poor Richard's Almanack*, 1737, "Benjamin Franklin's Famous Quotes," The Franklin Institute, www.fi.edu/benjamin-franklin/famous-quotes.

## CHAPTER 14: CHERYL BACHELDER

1. "The Gallup Q12 Employee Engagement Questionnaire," *HR Magazine*, May 1, 2010, www.shrm.org/hr-today/news /hr-magazine/pages/0510fox3.aspx.

## CHAPTER 17: A CHARGE

1. Galatians 5:22–23, 25.

## THIRTY-DAY EPIC PLAN

1. This EPIC Plan was designed to function on a week-by-week basis and is meant to be more of a map than a rigid program. It can be completed in one month, four weeks, thirty days, or for the overachievers out there, yes, even twenty-eight days. My hope for you, though, is that these questions, tactics, and goals will help guide you through the beginning of whatever God has called you to inherit and steward in this season.

# *Give Life to Those You Lead*

**TYLER REAGIN** knows the importance of identity-based leadership. His passion is empowering others to become confident leaders who infuse their team and organization with life, purpose, and vibrancy.

This is your chance to release the life-giver within you while leaving a legacy of eternal significance. That's the promise and power of *The Life-Giving Leader*.